Advocate for Music!

Blackwood

ADVOCATE FOR MUSIC!

A Guide to User-Friendly Strategies

Lynn M. Brinckmeyer

OXFORD
UNIVERSITY PRESS

OXFORD
UNIVERSITY PRESS

Oxford University Press is a department of the University of Oxford. It furthers
the University's objective of excellence in research, scholarship, and education
by publishing worldwide. Oxford is a registered trade mark of Oxford University
Press in the UK and certain other countries.

Published in the United States of America by Oxford University Press
198 Madison Avenue, New York, NY 10016, United States of America.

Library of Congress Cataloging-in-Publication Data
Names: Brinckmeyer, Lynn M.
Title: Advocate for music! : a guide to user-friendly strategies / Lynn M. Brinckmeyer.
Description: Oxford ; New York : Oxford University Press, [2016] | Includes
bibliographical references and index.
Identifiers: LCCN 2015030583| ISBN 978–0–19–021914–7 (cloth : alk. paper) |
ISBN 978–0–19–021915–4 (pbk. : alk. paper)
Subjects: LCSH: Music—Instruction and study—Political aspects. |
Music—Instruction and study—Finance.
Classification: LCC MT1.B775 A38 2016 | DDC 780.71—dc23
LC record available at http://lccn.loc.gov/2015030583

9 8 7 6 5 4 3 2 1
Printed in Canada by Webcom

This book is dedicated to my first-grade music teacher, Mrs. Davis, and to my students.

CONTENTS

PREFACE

WHAT, WHY, WHO, HOW, WHERE, WHEN

Music advocacy is an important current issue for our profession because music programs and other fine arts programs are slowly being squeezed out of the school day in public school districts across the United States. An unfunded mandate, known as No Child Left Behind, seriously eroded access to learning through the arts. Arts programs have experienced numerous cuts in funding and class instruction time. Some programs have been moved to the early morning, before regularly scheduled classes begin. Others have been pushed to the late afternoon following the last period, or eliminated entirely.

Most music educators are often so busy that they have little time to focus on advocacy. Their schedules fill up every moment of the day, evening, and weekend. Although the subject of music advocacy is often discussed in books used for university courses in music education methods, the actual number of books dedicated to the subject is quite small. The purpose of this book is to provide compelling information to encourage and enable teachers, preservice teachers, and parents to educate local, state, and national decision makers on behalf of music education. This text provides guidance and strategies for different levels of involvement in music advocacy. As a comprehensive document that includes a broad range of issues about music advocacy, it offers numerous strategies, materials, and models to advocate for music education. The five chapters are structured to answer the following questions in detail:

1. What is advocacy?
2. Why focus on advocacy?
3. Who can participate and where should we advocate?
4. How does one advocate?
5. When should we advocate?

(An extensive list of materials and resources are included in the appendices section following the final chapter.)

Due to the complexity of the profession of music education and the human psyche, a one-size-fits-all book fails to address all issues and situations in advocating for music education. Even so, this book provides a variety of strategies and suggestions for numerous circumstances. I am grateful to the National Association for Music Education (NAfME/formerly Music Educators National Conference [MENC]) for granting me permission to share its documents and resources. Providing documents and resources is only the first step, however, because people often require clarification on how to use the materials. Therefore, Chapter 4 lists numerous ways to use the letters, scripts, and other print materials located in the appendices section of this book.

Chapter 1 discusses various activities and stratagems that have been used in the past by arts entities and organizations. Arts advocates agree that advocacy strategies must adapt to a world that is morphing at lightning speed. Music educators no longer need to travel all the way to Washington, DC, to participate in successful advocacy for music education, although that can be a beneficial tactic. This book presents a brief summary of the historical progression of music advocacy activities by two of the most active professional associations in music advocacy: NAfME and the International Music Products Association (NAMM).

Chapter 2 shares compelling reasons for supporting and maintaining music study in public schools. Even though contemporary society utilizes music in nearly every aspect of life and people spend billions of dollars on video and MP3 recordings, music education is not always valued highly by the general public. Everyone who reads this book can access a compilation of links to cutting-edge research studies investigating the value and benefits of music education to students in the schools. This chapter includes anecdotal information regarding the positive impacts of music education and introduces NAfME's Beyond the Bubble Campaign. It distinguishes the differences between reactive and proactive advocacy and provides specific examples of both activities. Finally, this chapter contains a brief discussion about the status of music education in select countries across the globe. With this chapter, caring advocates can build a toolbox of persuasive reasons for arts education and contemplate the ramifications of a future society with limited or no support for the arts.

Chapter 3 presents a long list of prospective parties for music advocacy. Participants range from the music teacher and students in the classroom to national leaders in professional organizations. Every educator, preservice student, parent, family member, administrator, and community member can advocate for today's students to have access to high-quality music education. This chapter also explores an extensive list of associations and organizations to consider. For us to successfully advocate for school music programs and share our message about the value of music education for children and adolescents, we must foster relationships with those who have the potential to influence policy decisions that impact our children, teachers, schools, and community.

Chapter 4 is the most extensive chapter in the book. It delivers substantive information for the reader and serves as a handbook or guideline for the assortment of strategies and materials discussed. Many teachers are unaware that advocacy resources are available to them on professional associations' websites, such as NAfME, NAMM, or their state music education association (MEA). One advantage of this book is that it compiles and categorizes those resources and materials from multiple sources and organizes them in one location.

Chapter 5 outlines the best times to use various strategies for optimum impact. With guidance from this book, we can develop a consistent, sequential progression of proactive actions and tactics that share the importance of music study in schools. And those actions have the potential to positively impact the future of our students, *if* we implement them. Readers are reminded of the urgency for educating the general public, administrators, and policymakers, and they are guided to implement the ideas presented throughout the book.

The appendices section outlines assorted strategies on how to engage others in a variety of levels of advocacy actions. In addition to granting access to compelling research projects, it provides models of letters, webinars, printed documents, websites and contact information useful for communicating with local, state, and national decision makers.

RECOMMENDATIONS FOR USING THIS BOOK

Preservice educators, current music teachers, and parents involved with booster groups can all benefit from reading this book. Administrators seeking a research-based rationale for continued funding of music programs in the face of severe economic challenges can also access the book's useful data provided from quantitative inquiry. Because little literature exists primarily to help preservice teachers acquire advocacy skills before being inundated with teaching challenges in the first year, both preservice teachers and current teachers can benefit from the information and guidance provided in this user-friendly book. Usually preservice teachers know why they chose music education, but they are often uncomfortable advocating for school music programs because they lack the tools necessary to be effective. Both professionals and novices can successfully participate in advocacy actions at the local, state, and national levels by implementing the practical aspects of writing speeches, building a music coalition, working with administrators and parents, and utilizing quality advocacy materials and research findings. In addition to outlining details on ways to use the multitude of strategies in the appendices section, this book provides a brief historical synopsis about past advocacy for music and the other fine arts in schools.

I recommend reading all of the chapters in their entirety. After that, the book can serve as a reference and guidebook for action. Once the initial reading is complete, there are several approaches that can be utilized:

1. Evaluate the various advocacy actions and stratagems utilized in the past, and review their lessons, observations, and insights.
2. Examine the abstracts of the research studies included in this book. Closely scrutinize the studies that are relevant. Explore the web links provided for each of the original articles, books, or discussions. Investigate those new avenues of continued exploration about how music study benefits students and society.
3. Review all of the printed resources in the appendices section. There are multiple models of recommendations for written and verbal communication, such as letters, concert programs, emails, handouts, and flyers. Adapt and modify the letters or other printed materials as needed.
4. Inspect all of the strategies that are listed in this book and accept the challenge to personally utilize more innovative ways to increase advocacy efforts.
5. Watch archived webinars on the NAfME website for training in advocacy activities.
6. Systematically explore the websites provided in the appendices section and investigate the vast number of resources available on each website specifically developed to assist with music advocacy.

We have a responsibility to inform our colleagues in other professions and our community about the numerous benefits of studying music. Plus, we need to communicate the potential ramifications if music and the fine arts are completely squeezed out of the public school classrooms. This book provides compelling information about advocating for music education and serves as a guidebook for teacher educators, preservice students, and dedicated parents about the benefits of studying music. Use it to share multifaceted resources and ideas to educate the general public, administrators, and political policymakers about the long-term benefits of music education.

Readers can support music and arts education in a manner that aligns with their respective comfort levels and skill sets by using the various user-friendly strategies. The ideas outlined in this book can serve as stepping stones to develop plans applicable to each individual situation and environment. Approach the information with the same perspective you use when preparing a tossed salad. A salad bar is stocked with a variety of ingredients, and most people choose to eat some of the items, but not all of them. Every person has his or her own unique personality and skill set, so with that in mind, take any of these ingredients that have the potential to assist in music advocacy and leave the other items.

Advocates for music education can share succinct, research-based information to help educate people who have limited knowledge about or access to data about music education's benefits for children, adolescents, and society. This book communicates that information and brings together our best contemporary understanding of the benefits of music education and the most effective means of communicating that value in one book.

ACKNOWLEDGMENTS

My mother is my hero. Thank you, Mom and Allen, for always believing in me and for your unconditional love and support.

My dad was incredibly proud of me. I wish he was still here to read this book.

My daughter, Lanette, and my son, Willie, have been patient and supportive through all of the nontraditional paths I have created in their lives. Both of them, and their families, are precious to me.

I wish to express my sincere appreciation to Norm Hirschy, the three Oxford reviewers, Lisbeth Redfield and Deepti Agarwal for the time they dedicated to this project. I was privileged to learn from this process. The following individuals donated their time, expertise, and support to help with the journey of writing this book: John Benham, Michael Blakeslee, Patty Bourne, Bruce Bush, Michael Butera, David Circle, Kenneth Elpus, Nellie Hill, Tim Lautzenheiser, Mary Luehrsen, Debbie Montague, Jane Morlan, Marcia Neel, Nicole Yorty Papas, Paige Rose, Chris Woodside, and Sheila Woodward.

Finally, I want to thank the National Association for Music Education (NAfME), the International Music Products Association (NAMM), and the International Association for Music Education (ISME) for their continued contributions to music advocacy and for allowing me to share their valuable resources and materials.

ABOUT THE COMPANION WEBSITE

⊙

www.oup.com/us/advocateformusic

The companion website for *Advocate for Music! A Guide to User-Friendly Strategies* features supplementary materials for the book, including samples of strategies for advocacy at local, state, and national levels. I encourage readers to consult this resource to enhance proactive advocacy strategies.

Advocate for Music!

CHAPTER 1

What Is Music Advocacy?

Across the country, school districts are reducing funding for music education programs. Mounting pressures from high-stakes testing and increased focus on math, reading, language arts, and science often compel administrators to trim or cut fine arts budgets, class time, and programs. Music advocates agree that advocacy strategies must adapt to a world that is morphing at lightning speed. That is why teachers, preservice teachers, and dedicated parents can benefit from the information and guidance provided in this user-friendly book. The intent of this book is to serve as a resource guide for successful music advocacy. It provides long-range strategies and actions that require minimal effort or time but that still work toward the greater good for children and adolescents across the country. This chapter summarizes music advocacy activities and stratagems that have been used in the past by some music education entities and organizations. A few insights are also included about the historical progression of music advocacy activities by two of the most active professional associations in music advocacy: the National Association for Music Education (NAfME, formerly the Music Educators National Conference [MENC]) and the International Music Products Association (NAMM, formerly the National Association of Music Merchants). Each chapter concludes with a call to action to inspire and motivate advocacy activities.

A DEFINITION AND DESCRIPTION

What is *advocacy*? According to the dictionary, advocacy is "public support for or recommendation of a particular cause or policy."[1] Another definition of advocacy is the "act or process of supporting a cause or proposal, the act or process of advocating something."[2] Sometimes people confuse advocacy with lobbying. Advocacy consists of urging listeners to support a cause, such as asking for quality music programs taught by certified music educators. According to Chris Woodside, NAfME assistant executive director, lobbying is an attempt to influence state or federal legislation or the decisions of the president, vice president, or top officials of U.S. Cabinet agencies such as the Department of Education or the Department of Commerce.[3]

Early in my teaching career, the word *advocacy* conjured up the image of men and women, dressed in power suits, knocking on the doors of members of Congress in Washington, DC. As far as I was concerned, *they* were responsible for advocating for music education's rightful place in the school core curriculum. It never occurred to me that *I* should be an advocate for music education. Besides, I was too busy teaching my students to be bothered with adding music advocacy to my overloaded schedule. After all, in addition to teaching an extensive, required curriculum, I needed to make sure my students were prepared for our next program. Since then, I have learned that advocating for music education is my responsibility too.

My personal experience in advocating for music programs spans a period of more than 15 years in state and national leadership positions. I had the opportunity to visit music teachers and state leaders in 42 states during my terms as the NAfME Northwest Division president and as the NAfME national president. During my presidency term, I advocated for music education across the country as a keynote speaker, met with national legislators, spoke before a forum of congressional leaders and staff, presented advocacy sessions at state music conferences, and addressed the subject in monthly columns in *Teaching Music*[4] and *Music Educators Journal*.[5] Through those experiences, and with the guidance of past national presidents and members of the executive NAfME staff, I gained knowledge, tools, and strategies that I am anxious to share with teachers, parents, and administrators.

Music advocacy actions encompass a wide range of activities, from gathering thousands of signatures ratifying a particular issue to simply thanking parents at the end of a concert for supporting music education and urging them to continue to speak for a child's right to have access to music education.

A few examples of local advocacy activities include the following:

- Teachers, parents, and community members write letters and call decision makers or meet with them in local offices regarding a specific issue.
- Parents attend school board meetings and share recommendations for solutions to maintain music programs in schools.

- A music teacher meets with a principal and shares numerical data outlining how preserving a music program, rather than cutting it, is cost effective and beneficial for the entire school's financial health.

Advocacy occurs at the national level each summer when elected officers and staff members of the 50 state federated associations (music education associations [MEAs]) of NAfME gather together for the National Assembly meeting. All of the members of the delegation visit their elected decision makers at their offices on Capitol Hill in Washington, DC. For example, the elected officers and staff members of one of the NAfME federated MEAs, such as the Pennsylvania Music Educators Association or the Kanas Music Educators Association, set up meetings with their state senators and states representatives in Washington, DC. Quite often, those same MEA officers and staff members also visit policymakers in their own state capitol buildings when their elected leaders are back in their home states. Photos 1.1 and 1.2 were taken when the NAfME leadership visited their state senators and representatives on Capitol Hill. Photo 1.3 shows NAfME president Nancy Ditmer testifying at the House of Representatives in Washington, DC.

All of these examples are different types of activities at the local, state and national levels that support music advocacy.

Photo 1.1 NAfME leaders on Capitol Hill.
Photo courtesy of the National Association for Music Education, Michael DeMattia, MD Films, MAD Productions LLC.

Photo 1.2 NAfME leaders and staff visit a senator's office.
Photo courtesy of the National Association for Music Education, Michael DeMattia, MD Films, MAD
Productions LLC.

Photo 1.3 NAfME president Nancy Ditmer testifying at the House of Representatives.
Photo courtesy of the National Association for Music Education Michael DeMattia, MD Films, MAD
Productions LLC.

Advocating for music education in schools has been taking place for quite awhile. Even Plato was compelled to share the message that "Musical training is a more potent instrument than any other because rhythm and harmony find their way into the inward places of the soul, on which they mightily fasten, imparting grace."[6] Graduate students pursuing doctorate degrees in music education often read Edward Baily Birge's *History of Public School Music in the United States*. Birge details how Lowell Mason taught music classes without receiving any financial compensation for an entire year.[7] Mason was so determined to convince members of Boston's school board that students would benefit from studying music that he was willing to sacrifice his own financial stability for children in Boston's schools to receive instruction in music. Mason's dedication and passion for his students' access to music education took precedence over his personal economic goals.

NAfME elected leadership and staff began ramping up advocacy activities and funding near the end of the 20th century. NAMM also increased funding for advocacy activities. At that time, national leaders in music education voiced concerns about the ramifications of the unfunded mandate called No Child Left Behind, but the issue was not yet a high priority for the entire nation. Eventually teachers, students, parents, and business leaders began expressing their frustration and distress regarding the narrowing of the curriculum in public schools. June M. Hinckley, past NAfME president, testified before the Subcommittee on Early Childhood, Youth, and Families of the House Committee on Education and the Workforce on July 15, 1999. During her presidency, Hinckley developed an event that culminated in a book titled *Vision 2020: The Housewright Symposium on the Future of Music Education*.[8] Many of the best thinkers and researchers in music education met together in Tallahassee, Florida, to help chart the course for music educators and the music education profession in the 21st century. The complete *Housewright Declaration* is available in Appendix U.[9] The MENC Advocacy Activities Timeline listed in Table 1.1 demonstrates how leaders and staff members of NAfME increased energy and funding toward music advocacy after the year 2000.[10]

For discussion purposes, in the remainder of this book, music advocacy is divided into two categories: reactive advocacy and proactive advocacy.

Table 1.1 MENC ADVOCACY ACTIVITIES TIMELINE

Date	Personnel Involved	Activity	Outcome/Comments
1/3/1990	MENC, NAMM, NARAS	Founding Coalition for Music Education	
3/1/1991	MENC staff; support from NAMM, NARAS	Publication *Action Kit for Music Education*	
1/1/1992	MENC staff	MENC designated to write standards	National Standards as mandated under Goals 2000
9/1/1993	MENC staff, Wexler	Improving America's Schools Act	Worked on language to support music education, based on Goals 2000 and National Standards; act was not passed, became NCLB
10/1/1993	MENC staff, NAMM, NARAS, Arts Working Group	Passage Goals 2000	Final bill included "the arts" as a subject
3/1/1994	MENC staff	Publication *Music for a Sound Education* tool kit	
3/1/1997	MENC staff	WLC airing in Hart Senate office building	Featured Singing Senators, lots of staff; cohosted by Boxer and Hatch
3/1/1998	MENC staff	Statement of Principles	Drafted, signed by large educational associations
3/1/1999	MENC staff, Palumbo	WLC airing in Capitol building	Congressional attendance; Bob Clement, sponsor
3/1/1999	MENC staff, Palumbo	Statement of Principles in Cong. Record	Bob Schaffer (CO) sponsored
6/1/1999	MENC staff, Wexler	Bill to establish Congressional Recognition for Excellence in Arts Education Board	Supported by Cochran; not passed
7/13/1999	MENC staff, Wexler	Secretary Riley spoke to MENC National Assembly	Administration awareness of MENC, issues
7/14/1999	MENC staff, Wexler	June Hinckley and Joan Schmidt (NSBA) testified before House education caucus	Congressional awareness of issues

Table 1.1 CONTINUED

Date	Personnel Involved	Activity	Outcome/Comments
1/1/2000	MENC staff, Palumbo, Wexler, Arts Working Group	Passage NCLB	Included requirement that secretary consult with MENC; professional development programs, core academic status
1/1/2000	MENC staff, Wexler, NAMM	Resolution on benefits of music education	Submitted by David Mcintosh (IN)
2/1/2000	MENC staff, Wexler	Involvement in setting agenda for Arts Advocacy Day, AftA	Renewed our activities with AftA
3/1/2000	MENC staff, Wexler	Letter campaign to Congress	Involvement of members at National Conference
3/1/2000	MENC staff, Palumbo	Capitol Hill visits by leadership	Helped get appropriations for music teacher professional development, special contact with Boxer, Feinstein, Harkin, Jeffords, Kennedy, Pelosi
5/1/2000	MENC staff	Publication *And Music for All,* 1st ed.	
6/1/2000	MENC staff, Wexler	Sense of Congress resolution on benefits of music education	Became H. Con. Res. 266
1/1/2001	MENC staff	Meetings with USED key staff	Established meaning of "consultation" clause in NCLB
3/1/2001	MENC staff	"Kid's Party" on Capitol Hill	Worked with cosponsorship with NAMM, also Vh1; gathered many congressional offices
3/1/2001	MENC staff, Palumbo	Sense of Congress Resolution supporting MIOSM	Clemnet, Rivers, Tiberi, Holt, Davis, Blunt support; became H. Con. Res. 64
3/1/2001	MENC staff, Palumbo, NAMM	"Kid's Party" on Capitol Hill	Involvement of congressional members, staff, Sesame Street

(Continued)

Table 1.1 CONTINUED

Date	Personnel Involved	Activity	Outcome/Comments
3/1/2001	MENC staff, Palumbo	Introduction of "Presidents Challenge for Music Education"	Did not succeed
3/1/2001	MENC staff, Palumbo	Congressional hearing	Sponsored by Bob Clement (D-TN)
5/1/2001	MENC staff	Publication *And Music for All*, 2nd ed.	
7/1/2001	MENC staff, Palumbo	Grant from NEA chairman	$10,000 received for WLC
9/1/2001	MENC staff, Palumbo	Request for $4 million annually for music teacher professional development grants, with $550,000 set aside for MENC to analyze results	$2.2 million appropriated as new grants program for music teacher professional development under ESEA, Arts in Education section. Eventually became $6+ million for all arts
12/1/2001	MENC staff, Palumbo	Remarks in Congressional Record	Remarks by Karen McCarthy (D-MO)
2/1/2002	MENC staff, Arts Working Group	Response to Department of Education Strategic Plan	Influenced funding of Arts NAEP 2008
2/1/2002	MENC staff, Wexler	Letter campaign to Congress	Involvement of members at National Conference
3/1/2002	MENC staff, Wexler	Concurrent resolution regarding music education	Clement/Cunningham, Davis sponsors
3/1/2002	MENC staff, Palumbo	Board contact to members of Congress	Helped get first MENC earmark (03)
3/1/2002	MENC staff, NAMM	Congressional briefing	House education caucus briefing on MIOSM, music education
5/1/2002	MENC staff, Wexler	Remarks regarding music education	Read into Congressional Record by Slaughter
5/1/2002	MENC staff, Palumbo	Remarks in support of MENC	Language by Slaughter (D-NY) in Congressional Record
5/1/2002	MENC staff, NAMM	Appeal to Harkin to support IFMR research in music education	Appeal signed by Landrieu, Levin, Akaka, Breaux, Durbin; not in final appropriation bill

Table 1.1 CONTINUED

Date	Personnel Involved	Activity	Outcome/Comments
7/1/2002	MENC staff, Palumbo	Request for $2.4 million earmark for "Music for All"	Money not obtained; request was to implement mentoring and other PD processes for music educators. Related development was increase in professional development grant program to $6.5 million from $2.2 million, but expansion to all arts
7/3/2002	MENC staff	Request for $50,000	Money not obtained; request was for "music for minorities" program, supported by John Conyers
8/1/2002	MENC staff, Wexler, NAMM	Resolution designating 2003 "Year of the Blues"	Submitted by Lincoln, Cochran, Thompson, Frist; became S. Res. 316
9/1/2002	MENC staff	Appeal to Kennedy regarding collection of data on music education equal with other subjects	Senate bill language change; no eventual action in implementation
10/1/2002	MENC staff, NAMM	Appeal to Sec. Paige	Appeal letter from Miller (CA), led to Paige letter to superintendents stressing that federal money is available for education in music and other arts
3/1/2003	MENC staff	Launch of SupportMusic.com	At national press club; cooperative arrangement with NAMM
3/1/2003	MENC staff	Nomination for MENC for National Medal of the Arts	Not successful; had backing of Leonard Slatkin, others
4/1/2003	MENC staff, Gvox	USED grant	Grant for technology initiative ($50,000)
5/1/2003	MENC staff	Letters to USED regarding paraprofessional issue	Established issue; is now on agenda for reauthorization

(Continued)

Table 1.1 CONTINUED

Date	Personnel Involved	Activity	Outcome/Comments
9/1/2003	MENC staff	Remarks in Congressional Record	Remarks read by McCain (R-AZ) regarding OTA program in Tucsson USD
3/1/2004	MENC staff, Wexler	Resolution in support of music education	H. Con. Res. 380; by Jim Cooper, Duke Cunningham
4/1/2004	MENC staff	Request for resolution	Submitted by Tom Davis (R-VA) and Dutch Ruppersberger (D-MD); became H. Con. Res. 262
7/1/2004	MENC staff, NAMM, Wexler, Arts Working Group	Letter from Sec. Paige	Support for local use of federal funds for music programs
3/1/2005	MENC staff	The National Anthem Project	Had request for $2.4 million funding to Congress; not successful
3/1/2005	MENC staff, Arts Working Group	Defining NCLB asks	Included reporting requirement as unified request
6/1/2005	MENC staff	Grant from NEA chairman	Grant to support Liberty for All CD, linked to national anthem project ($50,000)
8/1/2005	MENC staff, Art Working Group	Work on data collection with department	Resulted in fielding of NAEP
9/4/2005	MENC staff, Palumbo	USED grant	Grant for analysis of model music programs ($50,000); book published
4/1/2006	MENC staff, Palumbo	Orrin Hatch (R-UT) spoke at MENC conference	Congressional awareness of issues, MENC
8/1/2006	MENC staff, Arts Working Group	Confirmed 2010 FRSS	Resulted in fielding of FRSS study
10/1/2006	MENC staff	USED grant	Grant for study of National Standards' reach into the classroom ($50,000)
2/1/2007	MENC staff	Publication *And Music for All*, 3rd ed.	
2/1/2007	North Central Board	Legislative visits, training	Increase of advocacy awareness among leadership, relationship building on Capitol Hill

Table 1.1 CONTINUED

Date	Personnel Involved	Activity	Outcome/Comments
2/1/2007	NEB	Legislative visits	Increase of advocacy awareness among leadership, relationship building on Capitol Hill
3/1/2007	Board task force	Publication "Music for All Students"	
2/1/2008	MENC staff, NAMM	Miller/McKeon draft ESEA	Maintained core status, Arts in Education grant programs, new money in Title I; draft stalled
9/1/2008	MENC staff, NAMM	Appearance of Marsalis on SupportMusic Call	Clarification of Obama position on music education
6/1/2009	MENC staff	Rally at USED	Presentation of petition to secretary; relationship building with USED
6/1/2009	MENC staff, working group	Meetings with congressional staff and Corporation for National and Community Service	Discussed rule making to optimize opportunities in the Edward Kennedy Serve America Act
6/1/2009	National Assembly	Legislative visits, training	Increase of advocacy awareness among leadership, relationship building on Capitol Hill
7/1/2009	MENC staff, NAMM	Appearance of Duncan on SupportMusic Call	Work toward letter, clarification of administration position
9/1/2009	MENC staff, NAMM	Letter from Sec. Duncan	Support for local use of federal funds for music programs
9/1/2009	MENC staff	Comments on RTTT fund regulations	Work for advocacy awareness among leadership (asked leaders to comment, using SupportMusic)
10/3/2009	MENC staff	MENC designated to write P21 standards with other arts organizations	Awareness vehicle for important (especially corporate) decision makers

(Continued)

Table 1.1 CONTINUED

Date	Personnel Involved	Activity	Outcome/Comments
10/8/2009	MENC staff, NAMM	Met with department regarding showcasing student performances	TBD; idea is to reinforce and showcase connections for music education at federal level
10/19/2009	MENC staff	Commented on common core to CCSSO, NGA	TBD
12/1/1987	Mike Blakeslee		Through present
6/1/1997	Palumbo and Cerrell	Lobbying, shared with ASCAP	Palumbo connected with Democrats, especially Obie; through 12/2003
3/1/1998	Wexler Group	Lobbying, shared with NAMM	Cindy Berry of Wexler connected especially with Republican/business interests; faced issues of preeminence of NAMM issues; through 11/2001
1/1/2000	Arts Working Group	Loose group headed by Americans for the Arts, League of American Orchestras, and in recent years MENC; includes museums, VSA Arts, Kennedy Center, others	Through present
6/1/2001	Paul Kerlin		Through August 2006
5/1/2004	Anne Ruach Nicholas		Through July 2007
2/1/2005	Larry Chernikoff	Lobbying, specifically regarding appropriations	Through 2006
2/1/2007	Chris Woodside		Through July 2008
6/1/2009	Hannah Sharp		Through present

REACTIVE ADVOCACY

Reactive advocacy refers to activities and issues that surface following an event or situation that threatens a music program's demise. Reactive advocacy is often more about damage control than creating positive solutions for the future. In other words, something instigates a reaction and causes people to focus their energies on keeping or saving music programs, fine arts credits, music ensembles or classes, and so forth. Unfortunately, reactive advocacy activities can create an adversarial environment for all involved.

What might be considered a successful reactive advocacy event may vary greatly, depending on the situation and issues of concern. In some parts of the country, advocacy activities may focus primarily on keeping a fine arts credit as a high school graduation requirement because members of the legislature are considering cutting the requirement. Other advocates may work to persuade decision makers to refrain from closing all arts classes in their elementary schools or collapsing all fine arts curricula in with the other core curriculum. Some advocates spend their time and energy convincing elected leadership that moving fine arts credits to a pass/fail grade in secondary schools has the potential for negative ramifications, such as reduced standards, and implies that fine arts classes do not matter.

The following story exemplifies intensified state advocacy efforts due to a critical bill slated to move into law. Arkansas Music Educators Association (ArkMEA) president Paige Rose alerted the NAfME leadership and staff that a bill was being introduced to a committee in March 11, 2013. If that bill passed, students would be forced to choose between studying visual art or music in grades 1 through 6. Although the bill was intended to increase autonomy for local schools and allow students to focus on one of the fine arts more rigorously, it failed to guarantee that the time currently mandated for both areas would be maintained. Students were at risk of even more reduced class time for arts study.

Using their Facebook page, ArkMEA created an action alert and submitted letters to relevant legislators urging them to oppose the legislation. Furthermore, NAfME submitted a letter to Senator Bryan King, who sponsored the bill. Senator King and other members of the Budget Committee were encouraged to collaborate with ArkMEA to revise the language in a new bill that would guarantee, at a minimum, that the current level of art and music class time would be maintained. During that same time period, NAfME launched a corresponding advocacy support campaign through its Groundswell Network (see Chapter 3 for information on the Groundswell Network). On March 12, 2013, Senator King contacted ArkMEA leaders and informed them that the bill had been deferred pending further discussions with ArkMEA and other stakeholders to edit the bill language. This example demonstrates the success of collaborative advocacy, which resulted from ArkMEA's vigilance and attention to the political climate in Arkansas.[11]

Although the original bill was deferred, Rose shared that another bill was introduced and quickly passed before further collaboration could be explored. The current legislation allows students to choose between art and music in seventh and eighth grades. Rose revealed concerns about the wording of the legislation because it might create some issues for certain schools if administrators choose to take it *at its word* and offer only art or music. For many schools, though, the new policy provides students with a needed choice for focused arts study.[12]

An example of parents participating in reactive advocacy unfolded in Kansas. Parent boosters in Kansas deflected a bill that would have crippled music education programs in that state. Kansas legislators proposed a bill in the state legislature that would have prevented school districts from using any state money for music programs. Jean Nye, Kansas Music Educators Association (KMEA) president, and David Circle, past NAfME president, contacted the high school band, orchestra, and choir directors and informed them about the bill, which was scheduled for a vote a few days later. The directors immediately communicated with their booster presidents and asked them to call their respective representatives in Topeka. The parents' interactions with the elected leaders were successful and the bill was withdrawn.[13] Music programs in Kansas are still supported by state funding as of the writing of this book.

Although it is vital to coordinate advocacy efforts in a crisis, it is more crucial to maintain ongoing awareness after an emergency has passed. Consequently, proactive strategies share the importance of music education and focus on ways to prevent an emergency from occurring. Therefore, now is an ideal time to move beyond the former template of advocating only during a crisis. NAMM's Director of Public Affairs and Executive Director Mary Luehrsen encourages us to remember that advocacy actions better serve our students as a wellness program rather than an emergency room.[14] Proactive advocacy strategies strive toward that end.

PROACTIVE ADVOCACY

Proactive advocacy encompasses those activities that anticipate or intervene before a negative situation arises. Meeting with elected leadership in national, state, and local arenas can support proactive advocacy efforts. Advocacy is more than just talking to elected leaders, although that can be an effective strategy to educate community members and decision makers about the value of music education. Preemptive undertakings in proactive advocacy emphasize collaborating, building community, sharing new information, and searching for options that support all of the constituents involved.

Changing the name of MENC to the National Association for Music Education typifies a proactive advocacy strategy. The National Executive Board of NAfME voted to change the name of the association in 2012.[15] The new name exemplifies a strategic move to increase advocacy awareness for music education in our nation's capital. Here is an example of why this move was necessary. Several times during my term as national president, news reporters placed microphones in front of me and asked, "So what is MENC anyway?" (They would pronounce it as "menc" instead of spelling it out as M-E-N-C.) I knew that I usually had 10 to 60 seconds to get a message across about the value of studying music. Consequently, explaining the name of our association used up some of those precious seconds.

Another reason for changing the name was to clarify and solidify consistent messaging necessary for branding music education at the national level. Most offices for national professional associations located in the Washington, DC, area include the word *national* in their association's name: National Education Association, National Association for Elementary School Principals, National Association of State Boards of Education, and so forth. Changing the association's name aligned our national music association with other prominent national associations.

During my tenure as the Northwest Division president for MENC, I was initially uncomfortable writing letters to congressional leaders and calling their offices. Much to my surprise, the staff members who talked with me were polite, friendly, and helpful. They thanked me for my input and usually followed up with an email or letter regarding my request or concern. As I mentioned earlier, I visited Washington, DC, quite a few times while serving in national leadership positions. In my first advocacy meeting, approximately 100 state music education leaders from around the country descended upon Capitol Hill to share their concerns and recommendations for solutions regarding the reauthorization of the Elementary and Secondary Education Act of 1965, Public Law 107-110, otherwise known as No Child Left Behind (NCLB).[16]

Proactive advocacy is just as effective at the local level. Nicole Yorty Papas is an elementary music educator who teaches at Derfelt Elementary School in the Clark County School District in Las Vegas, Nevada. I met

Nicole when she attended one of my *Kids, Choir and Drums* workshops in Long Island, New York. Nicole implemented a creative advocacy strategy by asking her principal for permission to hold a mini World Music Drumming workshop for the teachers and staff during professional development meetings at the beginning of a fall semester. Nicole wanted the other teachers and staff members to experience for themselves the process of music making, decision making, and problem solving that takes place in a world drumming class. She hoped that by participating in a music class together, the teachers would experience team building and gain an understanding of the intellectual and physical processes required to make music.[17] That fall, the principal and all of the teachers and support staff participated in a short world drumming class during each morning of the professional development training. They played echo-call-response ostinato rhythm patterns together on drums and classroom percussion instruments. The teachers and staff enjoyed it so much that they prepared a short meet-and-greet presentation for the students on the first day of school.

Nicole said that during the course of the year, teachers would sometimes pop into her class and play percussion instruments along with their students. She shared this quote with me from her principal, Greg Mingo: "That year was the best achievement year we ever had and I am confident that your team building return to school sessions were the catalyst for all that we accomplished."[18] Refer to this book's companion website (www.oup.com/us/advocateformusic) for additional examples of proactive advocacy events and activities.

Books such as Tim Lautzenheiser's *Music Advocacy and Student Leadership: Key Components of Every Successful Music Program, A Collection of Writings*[19] can offer proactive advocacy strategies too. Lautzenheiser serves as vice president of education for Conn-Selmer and is internationally recognized as a voice touting the importance of music education for every child. His charismatic personality and quick wit attract teachers and aspiring educators to his sessions at state music education conferences like a magnet. For years, Lautzenheiser has focused on advocacy through developing strong student leaders. His long-term strategy proposes moving toward fostering a community of leaders who thrive through the process of learning about and engaging in music making.

Author and speaker John Benham is another well-known expert on music education advocacy. His writings and conference presentations about music advocacy are compiled in his book, *Music Advocacy: Moving from Survival to Vision*.[20] Benham is credited with saving over $72 million in budgetary cuts to music programs. He helps us see music advocacy through the eyes of an administrator and provides a thorough synopsis and background on effective and ineffective advocacy strategies. His book offers much-needed insight for those of us who are not in administrative positions in the public school arena. Benham warns that music educators are facing a crisis, and he dedicates an entire chapter in his book to recommended ways to become a successful advocate.

Music advocacy is educating other individuals about the advantages of studying music. The key term here is *educating*. How do we educate others about the benefits of music study for our students? This will be discussed in detail in Chapter 4.

SUMMARY

The goal of this book is to provide immediate access to tools and ideas for proactive advocacy strategies. It may also generate a sense of urgency regarding our responsibility to build relationships with other music teachers, teachers of other subjects, parents, legislators, administrators, and other community members. Our message is that music is essential for children and young adolescents. Ultimately, we want to find a way to work together, because we all want what is best for the future of our children, adolescents, and society.

CALL TO ACTION

1. Examples of either reactive or proactive advocacy actions previously used in my school district are:
   a. _____.
   b. _____.
   c. _____.
2. List three types of music advocacy actions in our community that were successful in the past.
   a. _____.
   b: _____.
   c. _____.

CHAPTER 2

Why We Need to Advocate for Music

Why focus on music advocacy? Our profession is experiencing a crisis, because music education in American public schools could be facing eventual extinction. Music education exists to provide opportunities for all students in schools to participate in music study and music making. Engaging in advocacy is the primary way music education, as we know it today, will survive.

This chapter shares compelling reasons to support music study in public schools. Contemporary society utilizes music in nearly every aspect of life, and people spend billions of dollars on video and digital recordings. This chapter provides the reader with links to a compilation of cutting-edge research studies investigating the value and benefits of music education.

PURPOSE OF MUSIC ADVOCACY

Teachers, parents, and other community members are searching for alternative visions of education in today's public schools. What is the purpose of advocacy? Before we explore that question, consider the purpose of music education. Why should anyone, besides music teachers, care about music education? All humans want to know WIFM—what's in it for me. So, it is up to us to relate the positive impacts and benefits of music learning to others' lives. Only then, since resources are limited, will we have an opportunity to influence their decisions and priorities regarding future support for music and the other arts. We have an important message to deliver.

Successful music education relies on public support. As far back as 1997, radio celebrity Paul Harvey pronounced that the United States was spending 29 times more on science than on the arts.[1] Reductions in arts programs and class time are even more pronounced now than when Mr. Harvey's commentary aired daily on radios in houses and automobiles across the country. Unless we advocate for our children to receive music education, schools are likely to continue reducing the time during the day for children to receive music education so that they may fund other subjects and projects.

NARROWED CURRICULUM

Sir Ken Robinson is a popular English author, speaker, and adviser on arts education. Robinson speaks about the need for studies in the fine arts across the globe and has been featured on several TED Talks, which are global conferences sponsored by the Sapling Foundation. He maintains that education has three core purposes:

1. Personal: to develop students' individual talents and sensibilities
2. Cultural: to deepen their understanding of the world around them
3. Economic: to enable them to earn a living and be economically productive[2]

Robinson insists that not everything students comprehend can be compartmentalized into words and numbers, nor do words and numbers adequately represent all that we know.[3] Because knowledge is generated in ways other than just words and numbers, our profession has the potential to reach students who may be struggling in classes other than music. Many students thrive in the traditional subjects, such as math, reading, or language arts, whereas others face significant challenges. Schools should be places of growth, and music may create an environment where those struggling students can attain expertise and a sense of accomplishment. Music also has the capability of providing underserved students an avenue to experience achievement in a music class or an ensemble when success eludes the other parts of their lives.

In Robinson's book, *Out of Our Minds*, he shares this disturbing news: "Since NCLB [No Child Left Behind] was passed into law, almost half of the school districts have eliminated or seriously reduced their arts programs, and the associated teaching posts. . . . The arts suffered from collateral damage . . . [and] the tendency to look at a problem in isolation from its context."[4] Arts are being marginalized, and the voiceless are missing out on arts instruction.

American educational activist and teacher Maxine Greene urged that our classrooms should be places of nurturing and thoughtfulness in her 1995 philosophical writings.[5] She also stressed that it was important for educators in the learning community to be consulted in the critique and vision of education. As a result of more standardized testing, curriculum is becoming increasingly narrower and focused on only a few subjects. Enrichment activities are replaced more and more with competitive tests, leaving little time for developing higher level thinking skills or creative projects.

It is vital that we educate our children and adolescents by teaching to every aspect of the child. Increased focus on high-stakes testing puts pressure on everyone, from the youngest student in kindergarten to the school board and the state board of education. Unfortunately, high-stakes testing, with pencil-and-paper exams, only evaluates narrow and specific types of learning. It may be an efficient assessment process, but it often falls short when measuring students' learning, skill sets, and knowledge about music. The term *high-stakes testing* is used because the outcomes of those exams are the basis for administrators making important, life-altering decisions. Achievement in music class and other arts classes can be assessed, in some part, by pencil-and-paper exams. But those types of evaluations are limited when quantifying comprehensive music knowledge and skills.

Although this may be perceived as discouraging information, we can embrace this opportunity to redirect the trend and look for all of the ways to initiate positive change. Testing in public schools is a recurring subject in Central Texas. A recent article in the *Austin American-Statesman* suggested that now is the time to start talking about what happens beyond the test. A child's emotional education is just as important as academic progress, and students need to know how to work together. Furthermore, good teachers prepare students for life, not just for tests. Children and adolescents encounter real-world problems when they leave the confines of the classrooms, not multiple-choice questions.[6] They need problem-solving skills and positive coping mechanisms when things take an unexpected turn.

Back in 1990, Harvard professor Howard Gardner forewarned that unless teachers feel some ownership of their curriculum, educational efforts will have a dim future.[7] Gardner is known for his research on multiple intelligences, which includes music intelligence. His warning has come to fruition in some parts of the country. I received an email from an elementary teacher in Michigan sharing that several of her friends are retiring now. They told her that the constant testing leaves them little time to actually teach the children.

As we continue to explore the purpose of music advocacy, consider comments from Paul Houston's speech in which he discussed the unique benefits of studying music. Houston, president of the American Association of School Administrators, spoke at the MENC Centennial Celebration and Congress commemorating the 100th anniversary of the association.[8] He presented a series of provocative thoughts about the way the field of education prepares students for their future. He stated that children come to us with different backgrounds and abilities:

- Child 1 does not get it and struggles.
- Child 2 has the capacity to get it but does not use it.
- Child 3 gets the lesson even before we teach it.

Every child brings something to the table every day. Consequently, master teachers find ways to personalize learning because many of today's students do not have the resiliency to keep on trying till they understand. If students are never given the chance to fail, how can they learn and develop effective coping skills for adulthood? According to Houston, training makes people alike, and education makes them different. He said that education should plant the seeds of possibility for our children and give them information and tools that stick with them long after they have left our classrooms.

Also, Houston cautioned us to reframe the way we look at education because today's schools are designed for left-brained students. He warned that schools are paying attention to thunder while ignoring lightning. He used the analogy that we cannot fatten cattle by weighing them and said that current education systems are weighing children, not feeding them. Houston concluded by explaining that we need to work in the department of humanity for our society and center our decisions on the international need for creativity.[9]

WHERE ARE WE HEADED?

Many music teachers think of advocacy as an activity that should be left to the leaders in their state music education associations. Over the years, numerous teachers have shared their frustration that we should not have to advocate for music's place in the schools and core curriculum. We music educators know that our students learn more than just music skills in our classrooms. Not everyone is privy to this knowledge, however, and not everyone had positive, enriching music classes when they were growing up.

There is a sense of urgency among concerned educators and business associates that we all need to participate in music advocacy. If only a small, privileged portion of the country has access to music study, we will all eventually experience the impacts on our society. The more of us who advocate, the broader the audience we can influence. How will we be better off in the future if only the advantaged students of affluent families or those who are fortunate enough to live near a community music program receive music education?

Ponder this portion of Dr. Kenneth Raessler's keynote presentation printed in the *North Carolina Music Educator*:

> But finally, Mr. President, something in all of us is dying. In New Orleans music was silenced by Mother Nature, in Iraq music was silenced by a dictator and by guns and missiles and in the United States No Child Left Behind is gradually silencing music. We cry for beauty to replace the barbarism that surrounds us. Please do not be indifferent. . . . While our government tests, we teach; while our government spends excessive funds on death, we deal with life, with joy, with happiness . . . with the senses . . . with feelings.[10]

Raessler authored over 70 articles and contributed to several books on leadership, advocacy for music education, and excellence in education. He reminds us of our obligation as music educators to inform our colleagues in other professions and the community about the numerous benefits of music study.

PRIVATIZING AND OUTSOURCING MUSIC EDUCATION

Conversations at the national level of leadership in Congress have centered on a bandage approach to keep arts in the schools by paying professional artists to visit schools periodically and teach students music and art. Using noncertified individuals to teach children and adolescents produces a haphazard mixture of pedagogical practices and an inconsistent curriculum. What do most professional violinists know about teaching sequential, pedagogical strategies for second graders to learn music? Artist-performers usually approach their teaching from a perspective of playing one instrument or instrument family, not as generalists to cover all aspects of music education pedagogy in a class of young children. Professional musicians typically focus on how to play an instrument, how to listen to performances, or music theory. A professional trombonist may be a fantastic performer with innate teaching skills, but he or she most likely has limited knowledge about the child or adolescent voice and suitable literature selection or age-appropriate movement activities for a fourth grader.

Professional musicians who visit schools provide viable, supplemental experiences that complement the learning in the classroom, but that is not music education. It is preposterous to think that a published author can visit elementary school classes, spend 30 minutes to an hour with students each week, and expect that students will learn how to write intelligently. Is that sufficient to teach language skills? In lieu of systematic practices with a knowledgeable coach, would middle school and high school football coaches be satisfied if they were replaced with professional players who visited once each week? Just because someone is a professional, in any field, does not guarantee that he or she is also an educator. See Appendix P to review the National Association for Music Education (NAfME) Position Statement that was developed by music teachers in the field and that addresses the issue of noneducator performers in the classroom.[11]

Recent email discussions with teachers in a Central Texas school centered on one administrator's plan to move all of the fine arts classes to a pass/fail grade. This is one more step toward diminishing the respect for music instruction and solidifying the perceptions of administrators—and the general public—that music is not academic and therefore that music classes are expendable. Students should be evaluated and receive grades for their progress and contributions in music. Moving to a pass/fail grading system is a *bad idea!*

Including music education in schools is an essential component of American education. Consequently, it is our duty to provide a convincing, well-reasoned, and comprehensive argument so that other members of our society *get it.* In an interview with Mary Luehrsen, executive director of the International Music Products Association (NAMM) Foundation, she shared that NAMM has conducted research over the past 15 to 20 years with the aim of influencing public policy.[12] Luehrsen also shared that highlights of the most recent research findings are included in the complimentary "Why Learn to Play Music?" advocacy brochure, which can be downloaded from the NAMM Foundation website. Music advocates can use the research findings in this brochure, along with complimentary brochures available on the NAfME website to lend credibility in their conversations with parents, administrators, and policymakers.[13]

MUSIC FOR MUSIC'S SAKE

In our passion to convince others about the value and benefits of music study, we can spend an inordinate amount of energy talking about how music study helps students' success in other subjects. We also need to remind others about music's unique benefits. Chris Woodside, NAfME's assistant executive director, explained that the Broader Minded Campaign resulted from listening to the special and unique experiences music teachers provide for students. He mentioned that NAfME is evolving and listening to teachers in the field. Consequently, the key hallmarks for advocacy are expanding to include more details about the magical experiences that take place in classrooms.[14]

A brief summary of the Broader Minded Campaign follows: Music not only impacts academic achievement but also shapes the way our students understand themselves and the world around them. Music teachers know that music study and music making educate the whole student and provide:

- Decision making
- Grit
- Multiple ways of knowing
- Creativity
- Collaboration
- Communication
- Critical thinking
- Emotional awareness
- Reflective learning
- Process orientation[15]

Explore the following website to review additional details provided by NAfME outlining the focus of the advocacy campaign: nafme. org/?s=broader+minded+.

Music study helps develop the students *behind* the test scores because it shapes the way they understand themselves and the way they attempt to interpret the world around them. Studying music fosters discipline, motivation, and deeper engagement with learning. Music education programs nurture the assets and skills that pave the way for a student's future success, such as curiosity, creativity, collaboration, and self-reflection.

PERSPECTIVE OF EXPERTS ON THE BENEFITS OF MUSIC LEARNING

More and more teachers insist that it is okay to love music for music's sake and not just because it adds benefits to other areas of study in school. So let us consider the perspective of the following experts on the benefits of music learning: Elliot Eisner, Donald Hodges, and past NAfME president Scott Shuler are well-known national scholars in the field of music education. Stanford professor Elliot Eisner has written 17 books and lectured and written numerous papers on the benefits of music and arts education. He served as the president for the National Art Education Association and developed a list of "10 Lessons the Arts Teach," which align perfectly with the focus and message of the Broader Minded Campaign:

1. The arts teach children to make good judgments about qualitative relationships.
2. The arts teach children that problems can have more than one solution and that questions can have more than one answer.
3. The arts celebrate multiple perspectives.
4. The arts teach children that in complex forms of problem solving purposes are seldom fixed, but change with circumstance and opportunity.
5. The arts make vivid the fact that neither words in their literal form nor numbers exhaust what we can know.
6. The arts teach students that small differences can have large effects.
7. The arts teach students to think through and within a material.
8. The arts help children learn to say what cannot be said.
9. The arts enable us to have experience we can have from no other source and through such experience to discover the range and variety of what we are capable of feeling.
10. The arts' position in the school curriculum symbolizes to the young what adults believe is important.[16]

Eisner was an influential voice and leading scholar of arts education for several decades. He promoted arts education for arts' sake, rather than how arts help students learn other subjects.

Donald Hodges is known worldwide for his work on music education, music psychology, and the brain. He has authored 140 book chapters, articles, and presentations sharing his research findings. In his article "Why Study Music?" Hodges[17] outlined 10 understandings or experiences that are unique to music. Some of them overlap with Eisner's list:

1. Feelings—central to any discussion of music as a knowledge system must be the idea of feelings. From one end of the continuum dealing with vague, unspecified moods to the other end dealing with crystallized emotions such as grief or joy, music is intrinsically connected with feelings.

2. Aesthetic experiences—all human beings have a need for beauty and to activate their innate responsiveness to the organized expressive sounds that we call music.
3. The ineffable—precisely because music is a nonverbal form of expression, it is a powerful means to express or to know that which is difficult or impossible to put into words. Two of the most common human experiences that are frequently known through music are love and spiritual awareness.
4. Thoughts—musical thought is just as viable as linguistic, mathematical, or visual thought. It can be a potent means of expressing ideas and of knowing truth.
5. Structure—closely allied to the idea of thinking is structure. The human mind seeks patterns, structure, order, and logic. Music provides a unique way of structuring sounds across time, as well as providing a means of structuring thoughts, feelings, and human experiences.
6. Time and space—time and space are the *stuff* of the universe. All human knowledge systems provide ways of dealing with time and space. As indicated in *Structure* above, music is a means of organizing sounds across time. Although music occurs in *real* time, it deals more with *felt* time. Music, especially in connection with dance (bodily-kinesthetic knowledge system), is a primary means of experiencing space in time.
7. Self knowledge—music's role in intrinsic, and especially peak (transcendent, life-changing), learning experiences provides for powerful insights into our private, inner worlds.
8. Self identity—many gain their sense of self through a variety of musical activities and experiences.
9. Group identity—group identity through music is both inclusive and exclusive in that (a) music helps cement the bonding of those members of a group who share common ideas, beliefs, and behaviors, and (b) music helps isolate and separate one group from another.
10. Healing and wholeness—from more specific applications of music in therapy and medicine to more general interactions, music has profound effects on human beings. Music provides a vehicle for the integration of body, mind, and spirit.[18]

As mentioned previously in this chapter, the items listed here are not easily quantified. Still, that does not make them any less important. Hodges's 10 benefits encompass the essence of what it is to be human and how music enhances those experiences. Eisner leans more toward how music/art helps students learn. Both men highlight how music/art enhances life and learning, rather than how music/art helps in other subject areas.

A few years ago I visited South Africa with more than 30 other music educators. We were invited to stroll through the Soweto Township to meet some of the people who lived in an informal settlement, or shanty-town. We were greeted with smiles and welcomed into people's homes, even though their houses had no electricity or plumbing and were built with found materials, such as cardboard, discarded lumber, and scrap metal. We walked through the settlement and ended up at a building that housed the Soweto Kliptown for Youth (SKY), where over 300 orphaned students lived.

Children and adolescents drummed, danced, and sang as we moved past them to a meeting room in their dormitory building, and then they serenaded us for approximately a half hour more. Our delegation listened as the students sang traditional songs, and one of our teachers from the United States described the singing as a *tsunami of sound*. A steady stream of very young children poured into the room, sitting at our feet or joining the others who were singing. As I looked around, I could see that most of the teachers in our delegation were fighting back tears. We were traveling in one of the most beautiful countries I had ever visited, yet we were sitting only a few yards from the most abominable living conditions we could imagine. Still, we were greeted with unadulterated joy, singing, and dancing. At the conclusion of our time together I thanked the children and young adults there, on behalf of the delegation, and told them that we music teachers had much to learn from them about finding gratitude in our lives. These children, adolescents, and young adults shared their gift of music and showed us how to be better humans. As I recall that life-changing experience, I can quickly identify how each of Hodges's 10 understandings or experiences unique to music applies to these young people in the Soweto Township. Music helped them express their emotions about their situation and discover happiness and a zest for life.

Another music education scholar and expert is past NAfME president Scott Shuler. Shuler is a national leader in curriculum and program development. He served on the original task force that developed America's first National Standards in Music Education in the early 1990s. He cochaired the writing team for the National Core Music Standards published in 2014. Shuler's "Five Guiding Principles for Music Education" echoes Hodges's urging to teach music for the sake of music making.

1. Principle 1: An education in *all* the arts is important for *all* students.
2. Principle 2: Independence—music literacy, in the broadest sense—is necessary to lead a life enriched by music.

3. Principle 3: Independent music literacy can be defined as the ability to carry out the three artistic processes in music.
4. Principle 4: To achieve independence and transition to adult involvement in music, students must begin music study early and continue in high school.
5. Principle 5: High school music electives must address a variety of interests to attract a variety of students.[19]

By referring back to the summary terms listed in the Broader Minded Campaign, one can see that each of the items listed in all three documents by Eisner, Hodges, and Shuler fit within those categories of the Broader Minded Campaign. Music making and music study are multifaceted processes and they help educate the whole child.

Eisner, Hodges, and Shuler approach the justification for studying music from different angles, yet they all tend to agree on the principle that humans need music and arts in their lives. Without connections to other people, teaching is just another job. Master teachers pay consistent attention to their relationships with their students, peer teachers, and other people in the school community. We all want the students in our classes and ensembles to learn as much as possible in the limited time we have with them. Through the study of music, we teach people how to connect with their own emotions and function in life. Lifelong educators know that children and adolescents can learn more in settings where they feel safe and trust the teacher to give them opportunities to gain new skills and knowledge. That trust and feeling of security happen when teachers make the extra effort to go beyond the subject matter and form relationships with their students.

Without true connections, our relationships remain superficial and limited. It takes trust for students to be comfortable enough to risk making mistakes in our classes. A child may get wrong answers on written exams in other classes without other students knowing about it. When music students make mistakes, they are usually audible and public; everyone in the class hears them. John Medina, in *Brain Rules: 12 Principles for Surviving and Thriving at Work, Home and School*, agrees and insists that students cannot learn when they are fearful, because they have to be able to make mistakes to learn.[20]

On a professional excursion, nearly 60 music teachers and I visited several schools and one conservatory in China. A large general music class of fourth graders in Shanghai kept us mesmerized throughout the entire lesson. About halfway through the lesson, more than 40 boys and girls broke up into small groups and experimented on the Erhu, a two-stringed ancient

Chinese instrument. We watched student leaders emerge as different children in each group instructed those trying to play.

To the untrained eye, it would have looked and sounded like sheer chaos. An inexperienced person could have walked in during that part of the class and assumed that the teacher had lost complete control of the students. But we knew that the room was crackling with energy as the students taught each other. Even though the teacher only spoke Mandarin during the class, it was obvious to us that we were watching a master educator. For 45 minutes, all of the students were engaged in singing, improvising, sight-reading, moving, and participating in small group experiences. We did not need to know what the teacher was saying to understand what was taking place. The learning environment was safe and nurturing. During the time we spent with the students, they had the opportunity to experiment, make mistakes, and problem solve to find solutions. The teacher was a master educator and she gave those students life lessons through rich music experiences.

MUSIC EDUCATION AND HUMAN COGNITION

Even though Eisner's, Hodges's, and Shuler's rationales to support music study are convincing, policymakers insist on quantitative data to guide their decisions. The following research studies outline thought-provoking and compelling reasons for continuing opportunities for children and adolescents to study music and arts in public schools. Educators know that master teachers begin teaching at their students' level of understanding and what they care about. Teachers then guide their students toward unfamiliar information. Consequently, we may be more successful in educating decision makers if we follow the same process. Policymakers are data driven, so music advocates should provide data first and then share information, observations, and stories of personal experiences about students' success with music study.

BRAIN DEVELOPMENT AND MUSIC EDUCATION

Research exploring the relationship between making music and interactions within the brain are gaining momentum and national attention. A few prominent studies are highlighted later. This book is intended to serve as a resource and an organized compilation of information that is available for music advocates, rather than a thorough analysis and comparison of current research studies. Each of the studies in this chapter is presented and summarized to bring awareness to the types of investigations that are being conducted by experts in brain development and music education. Website addresses and web links are provided so that interested readers can access more specific details about each of the studies.

Harvard professor Karl Paulnack presented a keynote speech at a Texas Music Educators Conference and shared details of his work at Boston's Beth Israel Hospital in the Department of Music and Neuroimaging. He detailed four things that stimulate neuroplasticity in the human brain: music, physical exercise, play, and numinous experiences. Numinous experiences were described as mystical, spiritual, or religious—something greater than ourselves. Paulnack called numinous experiences *a recipe for creative brains* and explained that this was why musicians played music on the Titanic while it was sinking, why people prayed and sang after the devastating Haiti earthquake, and why congressional leaders paused to sing on the steps of our nation's Capitol after the 9/11 attack in New York City, Washington, DC, and Pennsylvania.[21]

Most people think that music is just for fun and entertainment, but it can also be deep, life saving, and essential. Paulnack shared that music captures our experience of life much like a container holds a liquid.[22] It allows us to retain our experiences and our feelings related to certain events. On any given day across the country, all four of the items Paulnack listed (music, exercise, play, and numinous experiences) are simultaneously taking place in countless music classes. Students are part of something bigger than themselves. They create and perform music. They play instruments or sing, use physiology, and have fun while making and creating music. Music learning involves physical movement, engagement, and enjoyment. Music has been the center of human expression longer than we have been keeping recordings of human activity. And people will keep on making music even if all of the school music programs disappear.

Neuroscientist Nina Kraus at Northwestern University works in conjunction with the NAMM Foundation to conduct large-scale, controlled longitudinal studies with Chicago Public Schools and the Los Angeles–based Harmony Project. She and her colleagues assess the impact of music education on low-income populations. Here are a few highlights from her research data:

- Everyday listening skills are stronger in musically trained children than in those without music training. Significantly, listening skills are closely tied to the ability to perceive speech in a noisy background, pay attention, and keep sounds in memory.
- Musical experience strengthens many of the same aspects of brain function that are impaired in individuals with language and learning

difficulties, such as neural timing precision, which allows differentiation between speech syllables.

- Strong connections exist between rhythm skills and prereading abilities in toddlers.
- Adolescent-centered studies show that even very basic rhythm abilities, such as tapping to a beat, relate with reading skills.
- Cognitive and neural benefits of musical experience continue throughout the lifespan and counteract some of the negative effects of aging, such as memory and hearing difficulties in older adults.
- Even a few years of musical training early in life improve how the brain processes sound.[23]

Kraus also collaborated with Erika Skoe to explore how music training in childhood impacts the brains of young children and reported their findings in the *Journal of Neuroscience*. They found that music training alters the nervous system and that those neural changes continue through adulthood after the training ceases.[24] For a more extensive explanation of the research by Kraus and her colleagues, log on to the accompanying website for this book (www.oup.com/us/advocateformusic). Detailed summaries are provided along with links to Kraus's research findings on the NAMM Foundation website.

Eric Jensen, a member of the Society for Neuroscience and the New York Academy of Science, detailed his research findings in his book, *Arts With the Brain in Mind*.[25] Jensen presents staff development workshops across the country, teaching educators how to use strategies that implement his cutting-edge research. Jensen stressed the major aspects of his findings in an article published in the *Kansas Music Review*. Policymakers care about the input–output ratio, or the cost per student per year against the resulting test scores. Jensen calls this the old factory model of education and insists that the arts are the driving forces behind all other learning processes, because arts nourish our integrated sensory, attentional, cognitive, emotional, and motor capacities.[26] A detailed summary of Jensen's book, *Arts With the Brain in Mind*, can be found on the *Harvard Educational Review* website (http://hepg.org/her-home/issues/harvard-educational-review-volume-72-issue-2/herbooknote/arts-with-the-brain-in-mind_61).

Deductions of John Medina's research on the human brain are outlined in his book mentioned earlier in this chapter.[27] Medina concludes that there are 12 different concepts about optimum brain functions and that every human brain is individually wired. A list of the 12 principles and more information on Medina's research are located on the accompanying website for this book (www.oup.com/us/advocateformusic). Music classes encompass six of those principles:

1. We teachers know that every child's brain is wired differently, so we search for multiple ways to teach all of the children (Rule #3—Every brain is wired differently).
2. If students are bored, they will not stay engaged (Rule #4—We don't pay attention to boring things). Music challenges the students and encourages students to continue to learn, grow, and improve.
3. To improve in music, students need to repeat the process of learning music over and over again (Rule #5—Repeat to remember).
4. Music provides multiple opportunities for repetitive experiences to solidify learning (Rule #6—Remember to repeat).
5. Students in music class usually enjoy being challenged so their brains are relaxed yet still active (Rule #8—Stressed brains don't learn the same way).
6. Students use kinesthetic, aural, and visual processing when they play an instrument or sing in music class (Rule #9—Stimulate more of the senses).[28]

As researchers continue to conduct studies about the relationships between music study, music making, and brain development, quantitative evidence is emerging to support claims that music study impacts learning in positive ways beyond being able to play an instrument or sing. Hopefully the data will eventually be compelling enough to reverse the trend of reducing the class time and funding given to music programs.

ACADEMIC ACHIEVEMENT AND MUSIC EDUCATION

Kenneth Elpus's research looked at music education and public policy. In a telephone interview, Elpus urged that advocacy move forward from an informed and empirical base. In a 2011 study, he and Carlos Abril found that music students tended to come from families with higher socioeconomic status and that students of Hispanic origin were underrepresented.[29] Also, Elpus analyzed high school transcripts from 10 national representative high schools spanning the time period from 1982 to 2009. During that time, approximately 34% of the students earned at least one full year's worth of credit in a music course.[30] However, his analysis found some evidence that Hispanic students, English language learners, and students classified as in need of special education services may have been systematically denied the opportunity to study music due to No Child Left Behind.[31]

The point of advocacy is to influence policymakers, so Elpus recommends that music advocates look at the world using the kinds of large-scale research that policymakers find convincing. He advises that advocates refrain from highlighting test scores, because there are preexisting differences, such as similar economic demographics, between students who pursue music education and those who do not. In his study "Justifying Music Education: Econometric Analyses of Issues in Music Education Policy," Elpus found that on the SAT, students who study music do not outperform students who do not study music once these systematic differences are statistically controlled. These results remained consistent in replications with other standardized tests when disaggregating music students by the type of music they studied.[32]

Elpus contends that students who choose to study music are already more likely to be successful and have certain advantages over other students. The sample for SAT populations is already skewed because it is composed of a population of students who plan to attend college. Findings from studies that focus on groups of music students' scores are bound to be based on class status and be more a measure of the parents' wealth. Insights from these studies can be informative, yet they are closely related to racial demographics. Elpus noted that music provides some developmental benefit, and that maybe the opportunity to study music should be extended to all students. Music study does allow for deep learning and social and emotional tracking. [33]

21ST-CENTURY SKILLS

In education circles, the term *21st-century skills* consistently weaves its way into conversations among educators and administrators. Daniel Pink, author of *Whole New Mind* and *Drive*, maintains that our future belongs to a very different kind of person: one who creates and empathizes, recognizes patterns, and strives to make meaning. Pink fears that 21st-century schools are concentrating on right answers and standardization instead of the creative skills they will need to survive in the evolving economy.[34] When he spoke at a special briefing before Texas legislators in the Senate Chamber, he urged them to consider that business and technology leaders seek creativity and innovation. Creativity and innovation are the keys to success for students entering the workforce of the future, so schools need to promote this by integrating the arts with other subjects.[35] Pink shared that *left-brain* dominance is obsolete and that the future belongs to a different kind of person with a different kind of mind—a creative, *right-brained* thinker. He contends that all of us need to ensure that our kids are being prepared for *their* future instead of being taught the way we were in the past. Today's business leaders seek out individuals who can provide novelty, nuance, and customization. Schools seem to be teaching the exact opposite; education is increasingly focused on routines, right answers, and standardization even though the workforce is no longer about those things.[36]

Johanna Siebert, director of Fine Arts for the Webster Central School District in western New York, corroborates Pink's recommendations. Twenty-first Century Skills are composed of the four Cs: collaboration, communication, creativity, and critical thinking. Music classes have strong ties to all of those.[37] Robinson, discussed in an earlier section in this chapter, shares that exact sentiment while speaking across the world. He contends that our world is spinning faster and faster and that organizations everywhere are saying they need people who can think creatively, communicate, and collaborate. Businesses need people who are flexible and quick to adapt, but they are struggling to find people to fill open positions. Robinson predicts that in the next 50 to 100 years, the children of today will encounter challenges that are unique in human history. To transform today's education systems to address the real needs of this new century, we must adopt a radically different view of how human intelligence and creativity are fostered and nurtured. Teaching an unbalanced curriculum will lead to a narrow, unbalanced education. If we are to meet the challenges of the 21st century, we need to move beyond the educational ideologies of the 19th century.[38]

Music educators possess an ideal vehicle to capitalize on the urgings of Robinson, Siebert, and Pink because music exists in humanity. It provides an ideal medium for creativity. In addition to teaching a sequential, quality curriculum, we music teachers also have the means to foster meaningful relationships with our students. We often work with the same students in classes for more than one semester and sometimes for several years. So we often get more opportunities to develop deeper connections with students than most of our peer teachers do.

VALUE FOR STUDENTS, THE SCHOOL, AND THE COMMUNITY

I was privileged to participate in an event entitled *Sounds of Learning*, which included testifying on Capitol Hill in Washington, DC. Mary Luehrsen, executive director for the NAMM Foundation,[39] organized the event in order for several authors of NAMM-funded research studies to share their research data. During his presentation, Gary McPherson reminded us that music is a species-wide behavior and that we have never found an ancient or modern civilization without music. Music is a tool to engage students in the process of learning *how* to learn. In fact, it is one of the last intelligences to deteriorate in Alzheimer patients.[40]

VITAMIN M

All educators, ranging from collegiate students ready to embark on a career in teaching to those who are on the brink of retiring, have the opportunity to continue the magic that past NAfME president Paul Lehman talks about in the following excerpt:

> Music is vitamin M. It's a chocolate chip in the cookie of life. There's a magic about music and that's why it has held such powerful appeal to human beings in every culture throughout history, including our own. Music educators have something that no one else can give them, and it's something that, once given, can never be taken away. It's the beauty and joy of music. We have it in our power to enhance the quality of life of every American through music. Let's make the most of this marvelous opportunity.[41]

Our subject matter is music, but the final product is much more than that. Music touches lives in myriad ways. It certainly opened up a path of personal joy and potential for me when I fell in love with my first-grade music class and my teacher, Mrs. Davis. I could not wait to get to music class, and if I got to play the sticks that day I was in heaven! Now that I am a music teacher I arrive early most days because I want more time to accomplish the tasks I have lined up. When I look at the clock during a class or rehearsal, panic often washes over me because the minutes evaporate so quickly. I do not *have* to go to work; I *get* to go to work. The master teachers I know are the same way. They love teaching so much that time flies by in most of their rehearsals and classes because they get to teach students about life through music. Now, many years after my first-grade music class, my most meaningful days are when I watch students beam with pride as they finally sing a challenging phrase with sensitivity and beauty. I love those "aha!" moments of spontaneous rejoicing when a child masters a rhythm pattern on a drum or barred instrument. Because of teaching moments like this, I stay inspired. Thank you, Mrs. Davis, for opening that door for me and inviting me in.

SUMMARY

I am a self-proclaimed music education junkie. I love this profession and I enjoy thinking about how to help others do the same. As I have accumulated years of experience, I have realized that my fundamental passion for teaching is to help students learn as much as they can about themselves, and music, in the very short time I have with them. It is that connection that I cherish the most, and *that* is why I stay in this profession. This chapter proposed a variety of answers to the question "Why should we advocate for music education?" Ultimately, and most important, we advocate because we care about students and their future opportunities. Somewhere and somehow, someone, something, or some event related to music touched our hearts. It ignited a spark in many of us to teach music. We want to give our students optimum opportunities for them to have that same experience. So we are charged with educating our colleagues in other professions and our community about the numerous benefits of study in the fine arts.

Almost all of us possess at least one high-level skill or area of knowledge, yet not every person is a genius in math, language arts, or science. Past NAfME president David Circle urges us to remember that we do not require students to take math or science classes because we expect them to be mathematicians or scientists.[42] Similarly, we have music classes so students can take part in a multitude of experiences, including the joy of making music, learning how to learn, and problem solving.

When students care about something, they learn more quickly. Studying music can be a transformative experience for students because people remember things when they are emotionally attached to the information. Taking music out of schools removes a subject that many students care about. Music study can provide a path to success for students who do not thrive in a typical classroom instruction in math, science, and language arts. Explore a compilation of additional resources, books, and articles that are listed on the accompanying website for this book to continue searching for answers to the question "Why should we advocate?" (www.oup.com/us/advocateformusic).

This chapter shares synopses of the most current research studies that indicate how music learning affects the brain and highlights compelling reasons to support music programs even in spite of limited resources. Although later chapters provide practical tools for engaging in advocacy, the core message of this book is this: Music education is valuable and essential. Daniel Pink, Ken Robinson, and Eric Jensen are some of our best contemporary thinkers, and they all stress the value and the necessity of studying music and the arts.

Music is pervasive in our society. Shouldn't our children be educated in it? Our students can stretch their imaginations through our medium because making music involves cognitive, social, and affective processing. By participating in music classes and ensembles, we furnish opportunities for our students to explore all three of those processes. As students build a foundation of music fundamentals, they can also broaden their own ideas for innovation and experimentation. Through music advocacy, we strive to ensure that *all* future students have an opportunity to participate in music education, regardless of economic status or demographics.

CALL TO ACTION

1. The three main reasons I think music education should be maintained and supported in the schools are:
   a. _____.
   b. _____.
   c. _____.
2. Three research articles I will share with my parents, peers, and administrators are:
   a. _____.
   b. _____.
   c. _____.

CHAPTER 3

Who Can Help and Where Can We Advocate for Music?

Teachers, parents, and community members across the country continue to express concerns about the diminution of quality music education programs in public schools. Who can help us in our quest to keep these programs in our schools? For us to successfully advocate for school music programs and share our message about the value of music education for children and adolescents, we need to foster relationships with organizations, associations, and businesses that have the potential to influence the policy decisions impacting our children.

Everyone who cares about children, education, and society can join the advocacy cause. All effort and energy is valuable. Participants range from music teachers and students in the classroom to national leaders in professional organizations. This chapter examines the purpose of partnering with organizations that are not involved in music because they can often attract the attention of the general public and policymakers, which helps in sharing the message about optimizing learning experiences and educational environments for students. We can educate our colleagues in other professions and members of our respective communities about the numerous benefits of music study. We can also communicate our concerns about potential ramifications if music disappears from public school classrooms.

Where can we advocate for music education? Advocacy efforts can take place in numerous locations in all walks of life, such as homes, religious institutions, schools, military ensembles, community organizations, local businesses, state elected offices, and national elected offices. Members of the music business community, including music publishers and companies that craft music instruments, and companies that supply other music education materials can join the advocacy movement, because these organizations have the potential to reach individuals beyond the public school and arts community. This chapter identifies individuals, associations, organizations, and institutions that can increase the impact of our music advocacy efforts. It provides access to an extensive list of associations that either support the study of music or have the potential to learn about the benefits of studying music. This chapter is intended to bring awareness to the many individuals who can participate in advocacy activities and the different varieties of organizations and associations that are potential advocates. The purpose of this book is to serve as an organized resource and compilation of materials and ideas.

WHO CAN HELP?

The first of many challenges we face when we advocate for music education is knowing who to approach. One way to start is by speaking with elected leaders and the staff and members of various organizations. Organizations and committees associated with schools may include booster organizations and parent–teacher associations. In addition to local, state, and national leaders, those who can benefit from learning more about the value of studying music in schools include school board members, elected legislators, principals, superintendents, peer teachers, athletic coaches, parents, business professionals, community members, and senior citizens.

Explore associations in neighboring communities to find those leaders who will join forces to support music education. Professional symphony orchestras, professional music ensembles, music businesses, music publishers, businesses associated with the sale of arts-related items, performers of popular music and their agents, and the recording industry all offer possible options for collaboration about music education. Collaborating with local churches, synagogues, Elks Lodges, Toastmasters, Rotary Clubs, and Kiwanis Clubs may be another option.

OUR BEST ADVOCATES ARE PARENTS

We can all pull together and take an active role in advocacy activities. Ideally, music students and their parents, or other family members, will be the most effective advocates for any music program. Teachers who deliver quality music instruction build an infrastructure of parents who strongly support music study for their children and community. Peer teachers, athletic coaches, administrative staff, janitorial staff, food service staff, and parents all share the desire to create the best learning environment possible for students. We music educators are charged with the responsibility to provide a positive learning environment that includes a high-quality, sequential, standards-based music education. A word of caution, though: The most articulate advocacy materials in the world are of little use for protecting any program if the music instruction is haphazard or subpar.

Parent booster groups are a valuable and influential resource for music advocacy. In Chapter 1, we learned about a success story in Kansas because of the active participation by a parent booster organization. Benham, from Chapter 1, devoted an entire chapter in *Music Advocacy: Moving From Survival to Vision* to explain how parents can use his system to create a music coalition.[1] He describes the reasons that a music coalition has more power than an individual. Furthermore, Benham outlines in great detail how to set up the most effective committees within the coalition. Ideally, these committees would address communication systems, administrative liaisons, statistics and finance, and philosophy and curriculum. A link to Benham's work is provided on the companion website for this book (www.oup.com/us/advocateformusic).

ALLIES FOR MUSIC EDUCATION AND THE ARTS

We music educators have strong allies in Daniel Pink[2] and Sir Ken Robinson.[3] As previously mentioned in Chapter 2, both of these gentlemen are published authors and are highly respected in the field of education, with significant influence beyond the constructs of our profession. They have the notoriety and national exposure to help educate and advocate to a much larger audience than most music teachers. They are both quite vocal about the need for music study to provide our younger generations the optimum skills necessary to survive and thrive in our changing world. Clout and national exposure offers both of these gentlemen credibility with audiences comprised of people less familiar with music education.

Dan Pink is an internationally known author who sings the praises of *learning how to learn* through artistic experiences.[4] Refer back to Chapter 2 to review his recommendations. Author and speaker Sir Ken Robinson speaks at conventions and meetings across the country about all subjects.

In one of his TED Talks, Robinson stresses the need to study arts and music to stay current and compete in today's global society.[5] Chapter 1 introduced author and nationally sought after clinician Tim Lautzenheiser. Dr. Tim has long been known for his ability to mix humor with serious content when speaking at national and international band festivals, leadership events, and state music education association (MEA) conferences.[6] He reminds us that the future of music education largely depends on developing outstanding student leaders in the music classroom. A ballroom full of marching band students heard a similar message at the banquet prior to the 2009 All American Marching Band in San Antonio, Texas.[7] Most of the young men and women in that national honor band already had a long list of outstanding achievements on their impressive resumes. But, according to the army general keynote speaker, their notable accomplishments were not nearly as vital to their potential success as the type of people they were and the people they aspired to become in the future. He encouraged them to be the best they could be. Several students and parents were still talking about his message long after the dinner was over. These students honed their musical skills as they learned about leadership and developing character.

Pink, Robinson, and Lautzenheiser, are some of our most prominent advocates. By embracing and distributing messages from such nationally and internationally respected music advocates, we add another layer of credibility when we urge decision makers to provide quality music education for children in our nation's public schools. Music education association leaders often invite speakers such as these three gentlemen to initiate thought-provoking conversations about music advocacy with their members.

GENERAL PUBLIC

Through the years, various conversations with people in other fields, including some of my own family members, have informed me that most people think teaching is an easy job that allows people to go home at 3:00 p.m. and spend their summers lounging by the pool. A teacher's perspective is much different. After students leave their classrooms, educators of all subjects spend their time attending meetings, grading assignments, answering electronic correspondence, serving on committees, filling out paperwork, talking to parents, researching better ways to engage their students, and writing or refining lesson plans. Music teachers are also fine-tuning their conducting skills, practicing on their respective performance instruments, learning music for future rehearsals, performing concerts or programs, and teaching private lessons to students.

For as long as I have been involved in music education, music teachers have expressed frustration that teaching and learning music are not taken seriously or considered a part of the core curriculum in schools. Pause for a moment to think about how music is often perceived in the world of non-musicians. Five terms that we music educators might use in describing music classes in public schools are *rigorous, focus, problem solving, multifaceted*, and *teamwork*. What five terms would you list? Which of those terms might the general public use to describe music in the schools? Chances are, there may be a distinct disconnect between the two lists, and terms on the latter list might include *fun, entertaining*, or *talented*. We are charged with bridging that gap and educating people who did not have the same opportunities with music as we did about the value of music study. To do this, we need to learn what our colleagues in the general public care about so we can understand their perspectives and values.

Where will advocacy efforts reach the general public most successfully? Most people are curious when a sports celebrity or music celebrity is in close proximity. Star power creates attention, and using celebrities in the music industry helps bring awareness to our message. In the past, the National Association for Music Education (NAfME) and International Music Products Association (NAMM) have invited celebrities from the music industry, Hollywood films, national television, and national sports to collaborate in music advocacy. A young Taylor Swift enthralled parents, students, and teachers when she attended an event for the National Anthem Project in Washington, DC.[8] Her mere presence created a huge buzz and helped NAfME spread the word to encourage music making by all. Capitalizing on Swift's popularity and status allowed the message about the benefits of music study to reach more members of society.

Another example of using star power to connect with the general public is NAfME's "Why Music?"[9] This radio public service announcement series features pop, country, jazz, and classical musicians talking about how studying music positively impacted their lives and the value of music education. Announcements are produced twice annually to coincide with Music in Our Schools month in March and with the traditional beginning of the school year in late August. "Why Music?" has received numerous awards and targets adult audiences who listen to contemporary, country, classical, and jazz radio stations. A few of the artists who have participated in this initiative include Vince Gill, Faith Hill, Alison Krauss, Martina McBride, and Tim McGraw.[10]

EDUCATIONAL INSTITUTIONS, ASSOCIATIONS, AND ORGANIZATIONS

Educational institutions exist in all sizes and combinations and offer opportunities to advocate for music. Universities and alternative schools of all makes, sizes, and concentrations have popped up all over the country. Examples include colleges or universities, 2-year colleges, high schools, middle schools, elementary schools, preschools, day care facilities, elderly care facilities, public schools, secular private schools, charter schools, colloquial schools, online universities and training programs, and home schools. Many of these institutions provide formal or informal music training, and they offer potential avenues for building relationships with teachers and administrators.

Some associations and organizations that can potentially advocate for music education are not always closely related to music. Elected leadership in national organizations for superintendents, secondary principals, and elementary principals make decisions and develop policies that can either support the study of music education in schools or negatively impact those opportunities for children. Two associations that monitor and influence curriculum and policies in the schools are the National Education Association[11] and the National Association of State Directors of Teacher Education and Certification.[12]

MUSIC AND ARTS INSTITUTIONS, ASSOCIATIONS, AND ORGANIZATIONS

We can look to music education associations for guidance and assistance in advocacy activities. NAfME partners with a federated MEA in each of the 50 states.[13] Texas has two state associations, the NAfME federated Texas Music Educators Conference (TMEC)[14] and the Texas Music Educators Association (TMEA).[15] A complete listing of the NAfME federated associations, with accompanying links, is available in Appendix AA.

NAMM's Support Music Coalition[16] includes associations such as the International Society for Music Education (ISME).[17] This coalition was initially established to support music education in local communities around the United States. According to the information on the NAMM Foundation's website, their advocacy efforts now unite over 130 international, national, and regional organizations.[18] Teachers, parents, and community leaders who seek to improve access to music and arts learning have joined together to form this worldwide collaboration effort.

Other examples of active music associations include associations for band (College Band Directors National Association),[19] choir (American Choral Directors Association,[20] Organization of American Kodály Educators),[21] orchestra (National Orchestral Association),[22] elementary general music teachers (American Orff-Schulwerk Association),[23] applied-music teachers (Music Teachers National Association),[24] and music therapy (American Music Therapy Association),[25] as well as accreditation bodies such as the National Association of Schools of Music.[26]

Type in the words *music advocacy* in any search engine and you will pull up more than 78 million results. At the top of the list are NAfME Advocacy Groundswell[27] and the NAMM Foundation.[28] (Log on to this book's accompanying website to access links for each of these organizations.) The music community encompasses a wide array of organizations, and each of them has the potential to collaborate and share a unified message. Unfortunately, a scarcity mentality with limited funding has in some instances fostered adversarial circumstances between different constituents. Learning to collaborate and working toward the same goal is the only way we will succeed in the long run. A sampling of arts associations and organizations that actively support advocacy activities includes the National Endowment for the Arts,[29] National Art Education Association,[30] National Association of Schools of Theatre,[31] and National Association of Schools of Dance.[32]

MUSIC EDUCATION POLICY ROUNDTABLE

Working together will accomplish more than masses of people expending energy in many different directions. In addition to the associations and organizations listed previously, a growing number of organizations participate in the Music Education Policy Roundtable.[33] NAfME leads advocacy efforts in Washington, DC, along with NAMM and members of the Music Education Policy Roundtable. NAfME's Chris Woodside shared that many institutions were doing advocacy work for music and the arts, but problems occurred because of inconsistencies in the requests, which created confusion on Capitol Hill. NAfME and the American String Teachers Association (ASTA)[34] cofounded the Music Education Policy Roundtable to address this problem, and this consortium continues to grow in membership and influence.

The vision of the Music Education Policy Roundtable is as follows:

A music education advocacy and public policy infrastructure of organizations dedicated to ensuring the presence and perseverance of school music programs operated by certified music educators teaching sequential, standards-based music education to students across the nation.[35]

Current members of the roundtable are listed in Appendix CC. Review the mission statements and other materials developed by the Music Education Policy Roundtable by visiting the website accompanying this book (www. oup.com/us/advocateformusic). Anyone who belongs to an organization or association that is not currently participating in the Music Education Policy Roundtable may contact the NAfME office in Reston, Virginia to begin conversations about a potential collaboration.

PRINT AND ONLINE MEDIA

Print and online media are expanding so quickly that few people have the time to stay ahead of the most recent app, website, or tool designed for people to connect. In addition to local newspapers, magazines, professional journals, and books, new avenues for communication play a significant role in most of our daily lives. Robinson reminds us that today's students speak digital as their native tongue.[36] Our students enthusiastically embrace technology, so we must too or we will be left behind. Depending on our individual comfort levels and imaginations with the various media, possibilities are evolving to use social media websites for advocacy strategies, including YouTube, Facebook, Google, Foursquare, TED, Twitter, Amazon, LinkedIn, Instagram, Pinterest, and Skillpages. New forms of these social media sites seem to come and go with ever-increasing speed. These modes of communication open up new pathways to educate society about the benefits of studying music and to reach a much larger audience. We have just scratched the surface using online media to positively support music education.

With social media, we are not tied to whether or not a newspaper will accept and print submissions. By posting advocacy updates on the web, we are able to share our message with a broader audience. Encourage people to "like" photos and videos of music students and teachers (remember that parental permission is required before posting photos or video recordings of students). Even people who live in remote areas, with no local newspaper, can still advocate using these online resources. Online sites can energize others to make a better community for our future and offer current students expanded opportunities to learn.

Even though social media sites provide immediate access for reading and posting information, print newspapers are still useful for advocacy actions. Newspapers are more likely to print information built around an event, such as Music in Our Schools Month.[37] Stories about an upcoming event will attract the most attention if they feature local people or organizations. When submitting a story, include high-definition digital photographs and a contact phone number. Be sure to include the date, names of the people or organizations involved, where the event took place (or will take place), and the actions that occurred (or will occur). Some suggestions for generating news stories are as follows:

- Conduct a poll or survey.
- Issue a report on the status of music in our schools.
- Present an honorary award to a local government official.
- Hold a contest—essay, poster, composition, and so forth.
- Stage a special event—a parade, open house, instrument display, and so forth.
- Organize a tour of your school music department.
- Play a free concert.
- Conduct a workshop on music education.
- Arrange for a speaker at a community function.
- Set aside a "music career day" or "music career week" during Music in Our Schools Month.[38]

Explore the NAfME website (http://nafme.org) for additional guidance on how to speak with reporters, which publicity outlets to approach, and how to prepare and distribute news releases.

LOCAL, STATE, AND NATIONAL OFFICES OF ELECTED OFFICIALS

Some advocates share the benefits of music education by distributing the message with people who are elected to leadership positions, such as the mayor's staff and members of local and/or district school boards. School administrators, parent groups, peer teachers, and community members all provide opportunities for building relationships. Develop groups of individuals who can collaborate to change the mindset of policymakers to support study in music. A group of like-minded parents often have much more influence than they realize.

Elected leaders who focus solely on the people residing in their respective states are those individuals holding positions such as governor, state legislator, or member of the state department of education. Other elected leaders represent their constituents both in their own states and at the national level. National congressional leaders serving in these arenas often develop and enforce guidelines, rules, and laws that impact education and arts education. National-level offices include the Department of Education, Congress, the Senate, the Supreme Court, and national administrative offices. In Chapter 4, we will explore multiple strategies on how to educate and inform decision makers at the local, state, and national levels. Review the strategies and scour the appendices to build the most effective advocacy process. Then, consider putting the first few elements of your plan into action by contacting the state elected leaders who serve the local community, because elected leaders usually pay attention to teachers or parents who live in their district.

BUSINESS COMMUNITY

Business communities fall into two categories: businesses related to music and education, and businesses not related to music and education. Business leaders in nonprofit organizations, national chains, banks, eating establishments, and small local businesses are often willing to contribute financial resources to support a variety of entities: sports teams, youth community groups, summer camps, and so forth. Contact the local chamber of commerce to find out which nonarts organizations and professional associations unrelated to education or the arts exist in the local community. Investigate which local organizations and businesses might collaborate and help share the need for music education in schools. Offer to help them by placing free advertisements for their businesses in printed programs at concerts or displaying their marketing information on a PowerPoint presentation in the lobby before a performance.

We can utilize the influence of the business community, including music publishers, book publishers, people in the recording industry, and music performers. Members in these organizations possess the potential to reach an expansive audience that encompasses much more of the general public than most music educators can reach. This section of the chapter focuses on those business leaders who already collaborate to support music education. Bruce Bush, Hal Leonard Publishing's sales and marketing manager for education,[39] shared in an interview that business leaders are genuinely concerned about the erosion of curriculum in schools. We might think that leaders in the music industry only care about music education because their livelihood is based on selling music and music-related materials and instruments, but this is not always the case.

Bush stressed that most of the publishers that supply materials for the field of music education entered that aspect of the profession because they care deeply about students and want to support music education. Yes, they are responsible for running a viable business, but first and foremost, music businesses exist to serve students and teachers. Bush also emphasized that most people in the music business industry are willing and eager to assist in music advocacy actions. He maintains that most people enter the music industry for altruistic reasons and they truly want to contribute to society by supporting the arts, providing music opportunities for kids and adults, and creating jobs. They are quite concerned that today's schools may not be preparing students for the current workforce because of the narrowing of the curriculum.[40]

Many companies have stepped up to fill the void left in some communities where music education programs no longer reside in public schools. Businesses are teaching private or group applied lessons in their stores. Although this is helpful, it does not *replace* certified music educators in schools. Music businesses such as Hal Leonard Publishing all belong to NAMM, and many participate in the Music Achievement Council, a nonprofit organization consisting of music industry leaders who are dedicated to developing and retaining instrumental music students and teachers.[41] The NAMM Foundation has funded research studies for over 20 years to investigate the value of music study; its website offers an extensive array of advocacy materials to disseminate these results to the general public, music educators, and decisions makers.[42]

MILITARY

Military ensembles already play an important role in outreach for and making visible the importance of music education. The United States Air Force Band has a variety of ensembles: Air Force Strings, Airmen of Note, Ceremonial Brass, the United States Air Force Concert Band, Max Impact, and Singing Sergeants.[43] As part of its outreach for and support of music education, arrangements of all of the instrumental parts and conductors' scores in PDF format can be downloaded free of charge from its website. Tips from band members on performance, practice, and rehearsal techniques are also available.

Music education articles, grants, and games and music theory lessons are provided on the President's Own Marine Band's website.[44] The United States Army Band developed PDF files for its Music Master Classes. Classes range from French horn fundamentals to an interpretation of literature for a jazz band.[45] One of the United States Navy Band's primary goals is to help promote music education in the United States.[46] The Navy Band presents clinics and performs concerts in schools and sponsors a High School Concerto Competition and an International Saxophone Symposium. Chamber ensembles from the United States Coast Guard Band conduct educational programs for students in elementary schools through the band's Community Outreach Initiative Program. And the Coast Guard Band performs a series of age-specific concerts each year for students.[47] Links to each of these military ensembles are provided in Appendix DD.

COMMUNITY ORGANIZATIONS

Associations in local communities are another source for advocacy actions and building relationships. Members of associations such as the Rotary Club, country club, Toastmasters, Elks Lodge, Kiwanis, Boy Scouts, and Girl Scouts are usually volunteers who contribute to their local community. Many of those organizations offer scholarships for students, and they can be an active, collective voice for music education. Parent–teacher associations (PTAs) are active in many communities across the country and are usually more closely aligned with the school than other community organizations. Consequently, they are in an ideal position to create a coalition for music education. Other types of organizations tied to music making include youth music ensembles, community instrumental ensembles, barbershop ensembles, and community choral ensembles. Neighborhoods have their own personalities, so other community entities not addressed in this book may also be interested in helping share the positive benefits of music education.

RELIGIOUS INSTITUTIONS, CHURCHES, AND SYNAGOGUES

Religious organizations provide valuable resources for building relationships with leaders in the community. Music plays an integral role in most religious services and ceremonies. In fact, music in churches and religious institutions is big business, and certain facets of the recording, publishing, and education sectors cater specifically to religious entities by gearing their products and services exclusively to sacred music. Unfortunately, a church choir director from a midwestern state recently told me that he felt responsible for teaching music fundamentals and singing skills to all of the children in his church now, because music education is no longer taught in the area schools where he lives. Thankfully, he is a certified music teacher with many years of experience teaching in public schools. Regrettably, not all of the students in that community are as fortunate as those in his youth church choirs.

We all need and benefit from experiences in music. It is nearly impossible to go anywhere in the United States without hearing music in one form or another. Consider places where you encounter music while shopping on a typical weekend. We hear music in the car, in a department store over the loud speaker or on televisions, in elevators, on ring tones of phones, when we are placed on hold after calling a number, in video games at the arcade— and the list goes on. We can even hear music that comes to us from space via satellites.

In Chapter 2, we discussed the implications of failing to advocate for music. Who needs advocacy? Our students. So who can participate in advocacy? Every parent, teacher, student, and community member can potentially engage in activities. The next chapter offers ideas that even the busiest person can use to support advocacy efforts. An extremely shy person can find at least one useful strategy and still remain within the constraints of his or her respective comfort level and ability. Embrace this opportunity!

SUMMARY

In *The Happiness Advantage*, Shawn Achor[48] talks about Zorro and his circle of influence. At first, Zorro was a weak man with no outstanding skills. His mentor drew a small circle around Zorro. Once Zorro was able to defend himself from everyone and everything within that circle, his mentor expanded the circle. Each day the circle grew larger until eventually, Zorro defended himself from a room full of would-be assailants while swinging from a chandelier. We can use that same tactic in advocacy by beginning with organizations or people near us. Once we have learned from them and we have guided them to understand our message, we can either stay within that circle of influence or grow and expand our ability to inspire change.

We all benefit when children and young adults receive a rich, experiential education. Music instruction, with highly qualified music teachers, provides that. Contemplate a paraphrased version of President Kennedy's famous quote: Ask not what advocacy can do for you; ask what you can do to advocate for your students and their right to a quality music education. Whenever we approach a class or new group of students, we immediately strive to find out what they know and then look for ways to relate our curriculum to their life experiences, so that we can move them from what they know to a new world that introduces the unfamiliar. Teachers and parents in every state can utilize the ideas and tools from this text to inform and educate decision makers in their states and communities. Everyone can find a strategy appropriate for individual comfort levels. Some teachers may want to call or write to elected leaders holding state offices or national congressional positions. Some may want to advocate by sharing information with their parent groups or local community organizations such as the Kiwanis Club or Rotary Club. Still others may feel overwhelmed by the prospect of advocacy and not know how to begin. Explore the ideas in the next chapter for user-friendly strategies that will help people ease into music advocacy.

CALL TO ACTION

1. I will contact the following organizations to learn what they know and inform them about the benefits of music education:
   a. _____.
   b. _____.
   c. _____.
2. Identify the most influential people in your local neighborhood.
   a. _____.
   b. _____.
   c. _____.

CHAPTER 4

How Do We Advocate for Music?

D oes the thought of advocacy make you want to turn around and run in the other direction? If so, you are not alone. Almost all music educators I know are concerned about the reduction of fine arts programs in schools, but they are so busy with the day-to-day responsibilities of managing their own music programs and personal lives that they find little time to focus on music advocacy. Teaching schedules fill up nearly every moment of the school day, and professional responsibilities often spill over into the evenings and weekends. In 2002, the National Association for Music Education (NAfME) distributed the Music Education Advocacy Survey: Quantitative Summary.[1] After the data was collected, NAfME leadership and executive staff concluded that the association's members were prepared to get involved in advocacy but that they needed NAfME to provide guidance for them to advocate successfully. Since then, NAfME has developed a variety of tools and training materials for teachers to advocate for music.

By drawing on my own experiences and referencing other authors' research and observations, I compiled an extensive list of proposed recommendations so that even the busiest teachers in our profession can find one or two workable strategies. We build awareness about music education's benefits by taking incremental steps each day. Instead of feeling concerned and overwhelmed, these tools are intended to arm individuals with feasible solutions so educators and preservice teachers can find at least one activity to help advocate for students' access to a high-quality music education.

This is the most extensive chapter in this book because it delivers substantive information for the reader and provides guidelines for the strategies and materials presented. Through my experiences working with classroom teachers and preservice teachers, I learned that many of them were unaware of the advocacy resources on professional associations' websites, such as NAfME and the International Music Products Association (NAMM). One advantage of this book is that it compiles and categorizes resources and materials from multiple sources and organizes them in one location. For example, the reader can quickly access information on how to find current research studies, acquire convincing data, and strategize on how to educate decision makers about the positive impacts of music study for children and adolescents.

Einstein said you cannot create solutions with the same thinking that created the problems.[2] His observation applies to music advocacy as well. Teachers who have solid administrative support for their music programs may be less interested in advocating. Yet, expecting others to advocate and to maintain a healthy status of music education in the schools is no longer sufficient. What can each of us do? A better question may be, how do we advocate? We advocate by anticipating, problem solving, and presenting solutions. As I mentioned in Chapter 1, there are different types and levels of advocating actions, and this chapter explores those and includes user-friendly tips. Here are practical steps for proactive advocacy actions in the state, community, school, and classroom.

To get started, begin with the strategies that are the most comfortable, and then move on to the less familiar strategies. That is what great teachers do. They begin teaching to their students' current knowledge and skills, and then they guide students to build on that foundation and embrace new concepts and ideas. First, we focus on building relationships with decision makers and educators. Next, we aim to help music educators and parents acquire the skills and strategies necessary to respectfully share concerns when meeting with decision makers. Start building relationships and advocating close to home and in the classroom. Next, branch out to foster trust with parents. Access the support documents in this book, and find ways to participate in advocacy strategies that fit your lifestyle, career goals, and comfort level. Think about solutions that help both the students and the adults you are educating. Help them apply the information presented to them rather than overloading them with data.

TEACHERS

Regrettably, some music teachers may encounter situations where colleagues, parents, or administrators question the credibility of, or even the need for, a music program. Music specialists can contribute first by educating parents, administrators, and colleagues who may be unfamiliar with the true benefits of music learning. A music teacher in Alaska once told me that only 2% of the world reads music. If that is true, then we can see why some people believe that music and the other fine arts are expendable. Our charge is to relate to their world *and* strive to comprehend their perspective. We can accomplish this by saying, "Help me understand your view—provide me with the knowledge that informs your insights. What am I missing?"

Teachers are very good at assessing students and instructing them at their level of understanding. Still, we sometimes forget that adults often need the same patience and guidance. Simply passing out a pamphlet at a concert and expecting others to see things through a *music educator's lens* may be an unreasonable and unrealistic expectation. Individuals who were not involved in music when they were growing up may need to hear and see the benefits for their children multiple times, in numerous facets of society. I have heard that we need to hear new information three to seven times before we change our mind. That is something to keep in mind for successful advocacy. Remember one of John Medina's brain rules from Chapter 2: Repeat to remember—remember to repeat.[3] Our message needs to show up in multiple places—and multiple times. This process of educating those who have the power to make changes is at the heart of determining the future of music education.

Teachers who develop and maintain high-quality music programs provide credibility for the advantages of music education because students and parents experience those benefits first-hand. Music is a vital component of children's lives. Think for a moment about how much money is spent on electronic devices, downloads, and so forth for listening to music and watching videos. It is mind boggling! Most of the general population only consumes music. Instill in students the idea of *music making*. We can do this by delivering the strongest classroom experiences for students and furnishing a quality music-learning environment. Happy students and parents are the most convincing advocates and the most persuasive voices for maintaining any music program. Find out if the students who are not participating in performance ensembles have access to music instruction in your school. Consider offering alternative ensembles, which will help garner respect for music and may entice students who are not interested in band, choir, or orchestra to participate in music making.[4]

ADMINISTRATORS

We can be teachers for the administrators in our school community too. By building relationships around our mutual interest—the students—we can all strive to agree on what is best for the school community. One creative music teacher worked to solidify her relationship with her principal by bringing him to a state music education conference. He observed first-hand the level of professionalism and quality expected by our profession. Once the principal sat in on sessions for assessment, advocacy, and arts integration, he was sold on the value of music for the students in his school.[5]

According to Benham, proactive and collaborate music advocacy is the most effective strategy, especially when it is about learning and focused on the students. Music advocacy actions may be perceived as negative and less effective when they are:

- reactive or adversarial,
- about money or taxes,
- about conflict and power,
- about teachers' pay or benefits,
- about saving jobs, or
- about adults, or focused on anything other than learning.[6]

Guide policymakers to see how advocating for music is intended to serve students, instead of saving jobs. Share advocacy tips with parents because administrators often listen to parents more than teachers and school staff members. Teachers, parents, legislators, administrators, school boards, and community members all have something to contribute to the discussion. Strive to develop a new level of understanding from their viewpoints. Acknowledge the evolution of our profession. Revisions are necessary to adapt to our quickly changing world. At the meeting with them, strive to agree on answers to the following questions:

- What are the hot-button issues?
- What are our challenges?
- What are our shared principles and goals?
- What is the value of music education to all of our students?
- What is the value or benefit to our school community and society?
- What insights and types of data do policymakers consider when developing regulations about education policy and funding?

Help colleagues, parents, and teachers understand the challenges facing decision makers. It is quite likely that administrators, school boards, state departments of education, and legislators are unaware of the unintended consequences of a narrow curriculum in today's schools.

Administrators may feel pressure from a supervisor to increase focus on math and language arts, which often results in less funding and time for music study. How do we change or develop policy? Start conversations with decision makers by providing feedback oriented toward a resolution. We can share how a proposed change would benefit students in all components of their life, their education, and society. Ask policymakers to consider reallocating resources to schools that are suffering instead of removing financial support. Remind them, and ourselves, that we share struggles and commonalities and we are all in this together for the greater good of our students.

At a Vermont Music Educators Association state conference, Lautzenheiser talked about the top five things administrators care about: attendance, student engagement, academic scores, graduation rates, and better habits of self-discipline for students.[7] Talk about those issues first with administrators, and then share additional information about the benefits of music study discussed in Chapter 2. Understanding the challenges others face is key to developing relationships and building bridges with people who see the world of music education differently than we do. Respect others with different views, because our assumptions may be based on limited knowledge. Be mindful of the challenges and responsibilities of administrators, legislators, and other educational decision makers.

Music advocates who bring solutions to the table, as well as concerns, have a better chance of building bridges when they approach administrators. Educate administrators by distributing research studies, reports, and anecdotes. Benham emphasizes that resolutions should not include compromises or suggested cuts. Rather, he reminds us to stay focused on solutions that maintain the curricular and extracurricular offerings for students.[8] Maintaining this focus will help us advocate more effectively. Most important, we must frame our advocacy materials and conversations in verbiage appropriate to policymakers' needs. Decision makers want to hear about research data, statistics, and evaluation that highlight the cognitive aspects of music study. If they have never experienced the intrinsic joy of making music, the logic of music for music's sake is often insufficient to influence their perceptions.

NAfME's Woodside often visits Capitol Hill to remind policymakers to uphold music as a high priority. During his interview, Woodside mentioned that only *new* research findings pique the interest of policymakers.[9] He recommends that we present research findings from the past 5 years because anything older generates little impact with decision makers. Refer back to Chapter 2 for more information. Advocacy flyers on the NAfME website (http://www.nafme.org) can be downloaded for school boards, administrators, and parent groups and include the following:

- *A Guide for School Board Members*[10]
- *A Guide for Parents*[11]
- *A Guide for Elementary School Principals*[12]
- *A Guide for Secondary School Principals.*[13]

Teachers can use these printed materials to initiate a dialogue with those who do not yet value or understand music education's positive benefits for students. (See Appendices A, G, H, and I.)

We music educators know that there is more to education than basic skills in math and science and that music can be integrated into most areas of the curriculum.[14] More and more I hear a collective cry for a comprehensive approach to meeting the needs of all students, and the well-being of children is at the heart of every advocacy effort. Success stories and testimonials from students and supporters are available on many of the NAfME federated state websites[15] (see Appendix AA), the website for the NAMM Foundation,[16] and the World Music Drumming website.[17]

EDUCATE ELECTED LEADERSHIP

It is no surprise that arts education is a political issue. But before we start bombarding policymakers with a long list of research findings, it is our obligation to build relationships with people in positions of power. Past NAfME Southwestern Division president Luis Delgado[18] reminds us that all politics are local, and he encourages us to look for the local connections first. Elected leaders in our country are charged with making decisions for education laws and funding based on research data. As in our conversations with administrators, we need to search for strategies and information to help us understand the viewpoints of elected leaders before we expect them to understand our perspective. Joan Schmidt, past president for the National School Boards Association, is a vocal and active advocate for music education on the national stage. She notes that we will only be able to help decision makers relate to our concerns and challenges after we appreciate and develop compassion for the challenges they are expected to resolve:

> I believe that policymakers at every level enter public service with the best
> of intentions. ... Most policymakers are in elected positions, and they need
> to accomplish their objectives quickly, if they want to be elected to another

term.... Consequently, decisions are all too often based on a desperate search for politically appealing solutions to complex challenges.... All too often, music advocates feel stymied by the world of policy governance with its laws, rules and procedures. And those responsible for policy governance feel assaulted by demands for programs at times when there is no available funding.[19]

Advocate or educate—it is all the same. It is a process of finding strategies to share an important message and using language that the recipient hears and understands. We seek to influence the perceptions of nonmusicians who have little exposure to the world of music education. Jim Howell, past president of the Oregon Music Educators Association and member of the executive board for the Northwest Division Board for NAfME, notes that there are a lot of uninformed people making decisions. He asserts that even though those decisions are intended to be positive, the net effect can often feel like *friendly fire*. He shares that people being uninformed is quite different from their being evil.[20] Using that mindset, we can strive to facilitate the flow of information to decision makers so it is heard, welcomed, and understood.

Nurture respectful relationships with legislators, because people in leadership positions usually want to hear from their constituents. Advocacy is about increasing awareness of music education's benefits. Therefore, our goal is to advocate and educate decision makers about the value of music education and to share the emerging research data with those who are less informed about these findings. Matt Mathews, a lobbyist for the Texas Music Educators Association, affirms that there is strong support for teachers among elected leadership, especially when they hear from a group of teachers who are passionate. It makes an impact on them. Yet, some elected officials rarely hear from people, and consequently, they presume that there are no major concerns.[21]

COLLABORATE

Collaborate with others—unite. A music coalition has the most political power to implement a change, according to Benham. Parents who support a local music program can mobilize an entire community for change.[22] I remember Mary Palmer speaking at a Mountain Lake Colloquium in the early 1990s; she talked about how snowflakes are one of the most delicate objects but that they are quite powerful when they stick together! Be a strong advocate for your own program *and* your colleagues' programs. Refrain from complaining about any issues or individuals. Undermining a fellow educator or another program in the school creates adversaries instead of potential collaborators. Establish supportive working relationships with other educators. Define an ongoing effort and unite energies, ideas, and funding. Promote all educational opportunities for students, including nonarts opportunities. Participate fully and join forces. Seek a resolution to the question "What can we do to work together that will benefit both of our goals for our students?"

Coalitions work within the school, as well as at the national level. Woodside elaborated on NAfME's movement for capacity building and fostering community through coalitions. NAfME is the first arts organization to participate in the Committee for Education Funding.[23] Furthermore, NAfME and the American String Teachers Association (ASTA) created the Music Education Policy Roundtable, the first large national coalition that brings together key players in music advocacy. NAfME maintains a national voice and federal footprint in Washington, DC.[24] The roundtable focuses on the following:

1. Policy development
2. Federal advocacy
3. State-level advocacy support
4. Advocacy training
5. Music education advocacy public relations
6. Web content and support
7. Membership development[25]

USER-FRIENDLY ADVOCACY

Now is the time to take action, and there are a variety of ways to do this. Every individual can participate in advocacy for the arts. The remainder of this chapter is divided into advocacy strategies for the school and local community, state, national, and international arenas. Letters, scripts, speeches, and handouts can be used as models to expedite the process, and these items are outlined in the appendices of this book. Even the most novice teacher or parent can participate in these actions because many of them concentrate on merely building relationships with others.

School and Community

Help raise community awareness about the importance of music education. People may not know what an ideal music program should look like.

Give them that information in a document. Be specific, provide details, and develop a timetable to work toward a series of goals, one step at a time. Listed to follow are ideas and materials that can help with advocacy in the local school and community. Start by focusing on only one or two strategies:

- Ask your principal for guidance to understand the power structure in the school. Follow the *chain of command* when requesting changes or sharing concerns.
- Review the slideshow entitled "Making an Advocate Out of Your Principal: 10 Things You Can Do MONDAY!"[26]
- Appoint a publicity chair from the booster organization to keep the local public and administrators informed about the music students' learning and activities taking place in the classroom.
- Invite parents to:
  - Ask school board members about their views on music education and attend school board meetings to gain insights into the challenges and responsibilities board members are charged to manage and oversee.
  - Organize a parent group and work with the music staff to develop a mission statement.
- Submit annual progress reports to the administration to demonstrate the music program's accomplishments.[27]According to Benham, marketing keeps the administration and school board informed, and we need consistent, relentless, strategic messaging. It establishes the validity of music education as a core value to the community. Formal assessments give each teacher a more accurate picture of what the music program is really accomplishing too. Key elements in the report might include:
  - Faculty and staff: Summarize student-to-faculty ratios in each curriculum area. List honors, publications, and years of service.
  - Curriculum: Outline significant accomplishments of the various groups in the music program. List festivals and tours, accomplishments of the students, numbers of students to graduate, academic success of students, and number of students on the honor roll. Summarize students' completion of music curriculum competencies and performance events of the year (both cocurricular and extracurricular).
  - Student participation: List enrollments in classes and ensembles, average class size in each area, percentage of students by grade/ school, attrition rates (15% or more between any two grades is an area of concern), and results of exit interviews with students who drop music.

- o Economics: Determine the full-time equivalent employee value of an average performance teacher, summarize expenditures of all budget funds, and demonstrate the need for the budget for the coming year.
- o Music coalition: An administration liaison committee of the music coalition should prepare a report in cooperation with all of the music teachers; the committee presents an abbreviated oral report at a public meeting of the school board, along with a formal written report. Summarize the activities of the music coalition and its contributions to the district, including fundraising. Express appreciation for accepting the report and the past support of the music program.[28]
- Create a profile of current enrollments in band, choir, orchestra, and general music in your school. Determine the FTE (full-time equivalent workload) value of the music teachers. Analyze the current status of the music budget (average allocation per student in each category).[29]
- Define each aspect or component of the music program: curricular, cocurricular and extracurricular.[30]
  - o Review all music offerings in the district. Are there opportunities for students who are attracted to nontraditional ensembles (drumming ensembles, guitar ensembles, electronic music, marimba ensembles, gamelan ensembles, show choirs, barbershop choirs, hand bell ensembles, piano classes, salsa ensembles, gospel choirs, mariachi ensembles, garage bands, and steel drum ensembles).
  - o Prepare a fact sheet about the school music program; use statistics compiled from students in the school. Conduct a mini-research project for how your students' grades, test scores, or attendance rates compare to other students in the school. Share your findings with administrators and share research data showing the benefit of including music education as a core curriculum area.[31]
- Offer scholarships for first- or second-year students to study applied music with local or area teachers.
- Stay involved continuously and strive to be the centerpiece of the school.
  - o Build a connection with current students, coaches, office staff, nurses, counselors, and custodians.
  - o Get involved in nonarts committees.
  - o Attend sports events, other concerts, school art exhibits, pep rallies, debates, and so forth.
  - o Visit the faculty lounge and establish relationships with peers. Mistrust occurs when people do not know each other.[32]
  - o Have different ensembles or classes travel to offices of staff members and classes of faculty.

- Perform for various faculty, members of the staff and administrators on their birthdays.
- Present the faculty, staff or administrator with a card signed by the students, a bouquet of balloons, flowers, or edible treats.
- Collaborate with all arts teachers in the school to present a joint performance.
- Partner with a department in the school to combine energies for a concert:
    - The English department could assist with a performance focusing on poetry.
    - The history department could assist with learning about a particular style period.
    - At the end of the event, present a framed page of the performance score signed by all of the music students.[33]
- Attend budget meetings, especially when there is not a budget crisis or agenda item relating to the music program. Learn how the budgets work and share the information with colleagues and parents.
- Invite special guests, such as the mayor, or local media celebrities to introduce music performances or events.[34]
- Invite a state congressional leader to speak at a major performance where ensembles will be performing.
- Provide contact information for state legislators in concert programs and follow up by sending email blasts to parents with links to contact their legislators.
- Pass out copies of prewritten letters to legislators at concerts.
    - Use the models provided in Appendix D, Appendix E, Appendix K, and Appendix L that highlight the benefits of quality music programs and community support.
- At concerts and music events, pass out preprinted note cards with three bulleted points citing recent research findings supporting the advancement of music education.
- Include quotes or other supportive statements from national leaders in concert programs. If your state has a senator or state representative that has publicly supported music education, write and thank him or her for being a music advocate. Include a copy of the concert program with his or her quote or supportive action outlined.
- Send an events calendar of music performances and tickets for free admission to elected leaders.
    - Print a calendar of all of the music events, concerts, festivals, and professional groups in your school district. Send the calendar, along with a letter, thanking them for their support of music education. Invite

them to attend the concert of their choice and to speak at the opening ceremonies.

- Provide links in concert programs to access general session keynote addresses from state music education association (MEA) conferences (available on selected state MEA websites). (See Appendix AA.)
- Provide links to websites with information or video recordings encouraging music making by all. (See Appendix Z.)
- Mail letters to all school superintendents, principals, fine arts coordinators, and school board members in the district.
  - A brief handwritten note is as equally effective as a formal, typed letter.
  - Say who you are (parent, grandparent, business, board member, etc.) and why you are writing.
  - Thank them for their service.
  - Include a return address.
  - Include a personal example about your child whenever possible.
  - Use inviting language, rather than demands, to create collaboration.
- Pass out preprinted forms, addressed to the school board, at performances. Invite people in the audience to sign the documents and collect them at the end of the concert. (See Appendix K for a model.)
- Write articles for the community newspaper and submit photos of music students participating in positive behaviors.
- Establish strong relationships with postsecondary music departments and music professors in your state.
- Present an *Informance* instead of a polished concert. Document which national and state standards were addressed during classes or rehearsals over the past 6 weeks or grading period. Showcase the pedagogical process of how the students learn in class. Take parents and guests through a typical music lesson. Invite parents to sit by their children and have the children teach them a song, a drumming pattern, a body percussion pattern, or how to use mallets on barred instruments. Always speak positively about the school and the entire music program.
- Cultivate relationships with school board members. Invite them to attend a rehearsal. Pass out a copy of the lesson plans and demonstrate how the plans are connected to rigorous national and state standards. Reveal how music contributes to overall student success.
- In every concert program, newsletter for parents, or music program website:
  - Provide contact information for all of the school board members.
  - List all of the dates for all school board meetings during the academic year.

- Perform for a school board meeting, and then leave a written advocacy statement for each board member. Download a PDF from the NAfME website[35] specifically geared to inform school board members. (See Appendix I for a sample.)
- Present high-quality performances anywhere and everywhere possible to create a reputation of success and high quality.
  - At all music events, distribute a flyer highlighting the benefits of quality music programs and community support.
- Write short articles to parents to inform them about the rigorous curriculum students are learning. Distribute the articles via hard copy, email, newsletters, website postings, blogs, and so forth.
- Communicate your music program's success to the local media. Invite them to concerts and events. This is especially effective for towns with only one elementary school, one middle school, and one high school.[36]
  - Invite city leaders, such as the mayor or school board members, to those performances. Introduce them to the audience and publicly thank them for their support.
- Start a chapter for the TRI-M Music Honor Society.[37]
- Build relationships with local music dealers. Ask how you can help them. Ask them how they would like to be involved in supporting music education.[38]
- At concerts, provide a one-page information sheet summarizing major research findings that support music education's contributions to students' learning and the benefits to society.[39]
- Have students write testimonials about how music study has helped them in their lives. Print quotes on a handout and create a PowerPoint presentation with short sound bites from the testimonials. Have it running on a video screen before a performance or on a television monitor out in the lobby during intermissions.
- Invite students to complete "music makes the difference because..." and share their thoughts in concert programs, in school newspapers, and on banners around the school.
- Gather stories from students, parents, and community members to share with decision makers.
- Distribute a visual aid score sheet to parents so they can assess and provide feedback at a performance. This helps parents gain an understanding of the demands placed on students, and it provides a tool for them to connect with the learning that takes place in the classroom.[40]
- Establish a student-mentoring program. Pair up middle school and elementary music students with a high school student.[41]

- Set up an electronic system (phone-tree, group text, email, Twitter, Facebook, website, etc.) for efficient communication.
- Conduct more data-driven research to demonstrate to legislators and decision makers that students actually benefit from more music study and music-making experiences. Benham advises that more research is needed, especially in choral music to find out the characteristics of successful choral students.[42]
  - Investigate music's impact on learners' success and distribute the research findings to those individuals and decision makers who may not be aware of the benefits.
  - Distribute research findings through arts organizations such as Society for Research in Music Education.[43]
- Explain that more training is needed for content area evaluations for administrators. Provide models of music teaching evaluation and assessment tools for administrators and guidance for how to implement them. Contact your state MEA-affiliated association to find the assessment experts in your state. (See Appendix AA.)
- Review the items on the NAfME website under "What to Say" for guidance, because everyone's voice is needed if we are going to build and maintain music programs[44] (http://www.nafme.org/take-action/what-to-say).
- Explore various websites that actively advocate for music. A comprehensive list of websites is located in the appendices section of this text.
- Log on to the NAMM Foundation website to retrieve information for advocating at the school and local levels. The NAMM Foundation offers resources to enhance success with advocacy actions. The following materials are available in PDF format on the website and can be downloaded for immediate use:[45]
  - For educators: A Practical Guide for Recruitment and Retention; Tips for Success; Bridging The Gap
  - For parents: Why Learn to Play Music? Grassroots Advocacy Guide.[46]

State

Some individuals may be interested in advocating for music with state policymakers. Before delving into the suggested advocacy actions focused on building relationships with state leaders and influencing their stance on music education, consider that our educational environment of today relies strongly on quantifiable achievement measures to represent student learning. Still, data that indicate positive relationships between music and academic achievement are limited. Engagement with music shapes the students behind the scores and helps them understand the world around them, as well as themselves.[47]

People who are motivated to seek out information on advocacy issues with state policymakers can access updates and recommendations through NAfME and many of the federated MEAs. See Appendix AA to access a comprehensive list of the NAfME federated MEA websites.[48] Leadership and staff members in those associations, as well as other music education associations across the country, often have a recurring advocacy column in a newsletter or journal. Many states have an advocacy chair or staff person who publishes articles focused on music advocacy and updates on legislative issues in their respective states. Some states employ a full-time lobbyist who maintains a consistent presence in that state's capital and fosters relationships with their elected leaders.

Contact the state president or executive director of your state MEA to learn the most effective way to approach or contact a state senator or state representative. Find out who guides and facilitates the advocacy projects in your state and ask them for guidance. Ask the leadership how they disseminate information and updates on current advocacy issues and about their preferred process for submitting recommendations for changes. They may already have a specific process and materials established to expedite the process. Consider offering to assist them or ask them for guidance to advocate effectively.

Listed in this section are additional strategies for successfully advocating for music with state elected leadership and members of their staff. Decide which of these ideas best suit the current circumstances in your state, and your individual comfort level applying these actions.

- Contact a popular state legislator and ask him or her to sponsor your students to perform at the state capitol. If this is unfamiliar or daunting to you, contact your state MEA president or executive director, who may be able to provide guidance on the most effective process.
  - Ask the legislator to greet the students and speak about educational issues at the performance.
  - Document the event with photos and a short article in the local newspaper.
  - Submit a short promotional article and photos to the MEA advocacy chair.

- Review state MEA journals and websites to gain new ideas on advocating for music. (See Appendix AA.)
  - Submit an article to your state MEA journal and include excerpts from each of your students about why music is important to them. (See Appendix AA.)
- Volunteer to lead advocacy activities and recruit other leaders to help. Establish agreements with other organizations such as arts education associations, drama teachers' associations, teachers' unions, professional performers, professional orchestras, other instrumental ensembles, professional vocal ensembles, and arts councils. Lists of various organizations are provided on the accompanying website for this book (www.oup.com/us/advocateformusic).
- Present awards and forms of recognition to legislators, or a representative from their office, who support and protect fine arts in school.[49]
  - Submit a photo and short article to the local newspaper. After the newspaper prints the information, send a copy of the article and photo to the legislator or representative with a handwritten thank you note.
  - Review the Texas Music Educators Association's Distinguished Service Award to State Representative Jimmie Aycock as a model to consider.[50]
- Distribute copies of prewritten letters to legislators at concerts. Model letters are provided in Appendices D and Q. Explain to the audience why music study is beneficial to their children and to the community. Have attendees sign the letters during the concert. Place a basket at the back of the room to collect the letters as people leave the event or have student leaders gather them at the end of the concert. Mail the letters to the respective policymaker the next morning. Follow up with parents once you receive a reply from the elected leader.
- Pass out preprinted note cards with three bulleted points outlining the benefits of music study at each music event. Consistently remind the audience members about the benefits of music education. Encourage parents to write a short, personal message to state leaders. Collect the cards after the concert and mail them to the elected leaders.
  - Ask the parents to take extra cards to share with their friends and colleagues after they leave the concert.
- Send email blasts to parents that include links to contact their state legislators.
  - Ask them to provide their own stories to the decision makers about the three bulleted points provided for them.

- Short, individual notes work better than a form letter. Using parents' own ideas to develop the three key points is more effective. Encourage them to keep it grassroots, short, and simple.
- Display these comments from the parents on a PowerPoint presentation as the audience arrives before the next concert.
- Provide a timeline for submission and a recommended message for them to share.

- Follow-up and reflection are vital. When following up with decision makers, emphasize how important a specific action is and thank them for their service, time, and consideration, and for allowing you to share your information with them. Write a thank you card even if you did not get the result you wanted, because that action may plant the seed that builds a collaborative relationship for the future.
- Ask parents and students to write letters to government officials about a specific issue.
  - Richard Victor, music advocate and past president for the Pennsylvania Music Educators Association, says that 10 letters will put an issue on decision makers' radar screen, 25 will make them explore the issue, and 50 can change a position on an upcoming vote.
  - Many people speaking in a unified voice are much louder than an individual disgruntled teacher or a small group of angry parents.[51]
- Write or call the governor's office about important issues relating to music education.
- Find out when a state representative will be in town and schedule an appointment to visit his or her local office.
  - Personally invite the state representative to visit your class to observe students' learning first-hand.
  - Leave advocacy materials and contact information with the representative or his or her staff.
  - Follow up to thank the state representative for his or her service and time, and include a reminder of the invitation once again.
  - If the representative does visit your class, be sure to invite the local media and document the visit with several photos.
- Be ready to speak in 3-minute sound bites to policymakers. For example: "Every person must take math, yet only 1% of the population pursues math as a profession in the workforce." Decision makers at local, state, and federal levels are extremely busy and they have people vying for their attention at every turn. Practice a sound bite until it rolls off the tongue easily.
  - Thank the leader or staff member for his or her time. State the three talking points. Briefly explain each point and thank him or her again.

- Hand the leader or staff member documentation and ask if he or she has any questions. (See Appendix B and Appendix E for ideas.)
- Encourage your student officers to write to legislators and invite policy-makers to attend a concert performance as honored guests.
- Visit state legislators. Personally invite them to emcee a concert, narrate the performance (if a piece requires narration), or give a short speech. Provide a list of dates, venues, and times of upcoming performances.
- Contact your state MEA and ask for a list of points or strategies to utilize social media for advocacy actions.
    - Rally parents and colleagues to gather a tremendous number of "likes" on social media sites to create congressional buzz regarding issues about music education.

National

A few individuals want to advocate for music education with national policymakers. To gain a clear understanding of how to advocate at the national level, consider exploring the materials offered by the Music Education Policy Roundtable. PDF documents entitled "Connecting With Legislators," "Key Federal Education Members," and "Public Relations 101" provide valuable information and specific guidance for advocacy actions with national decision makers.[52]

Lautzenheiser reminds us that most people responsible for developing an educational foundation are committed to excellence and willing to listen to data that support a holistic, quality learning experience for every child. Nearly every legislative candidate wants to connect with people and takes his or her job seriously. Legislators are charged with the task of preparing students to embrace the responsibilities of living a prosperous, successful life.[53] Because parents and teachers now clamor for a more balanced curriculum, bring information to Capitol Hill that is translated into legislative recommendations and make the case for a well-balanced school day. Listed to follow are additional strategies for advocating for music at the national level:

- Investigate and sign up for Groundswell on the NAfME website to receive the latest updates and recommendations on current issues.[54]
- When visiting a senator or representative's office in our nation's Capitol, be sure to inform the staff members that you are from the legislator's home state. Most of the time people are ushered to the front of the line if they are constituents from home.[55]

- Participate in NAfME's Music in Our Schools Month activities during March of each year.[56]
- Sign up for advocacy webinars on the NAfME website and review archived webinars. Information provided on those webinars will help people to prepare for action when called on.[57] (See Appendix C, Appendix J, and Appendix O.)
  - Share successful strategies and actions. Let others know about activities, successes, and roadblocks. Report stories about your students' advanced learning or accelerated learning by sending an email to the following address: advocateformusic@gmail.com. Those stories will be posted periodically to the website that accompanies this book (www.oup.com/us/advocateformusic).

International

The International Society for Music Education (ISME) created an Advocacy Standing Committee for the purpose of identifying and creating opportunities to advocate on behalf of music education in international forums across the globe. The Advocacy Standing Committee's mission statement emphasizes the importance of including music education for every child. Specific details about the work of the Advocacy Standing Committee are available on the ISME's website.[58] Interested parties can review the following strategies for advocating for music at an international level:

- Explore archived blogs and webinars on ISME's website addressing advocacy for music education across the world:
  - EMC Strategy—Music and Politics, Music Education
  - Professor Grahm Welch on BBC's *The Other One Show* (National Sing Up Day)
  - School Singing Can Boost Children's Well-Being
  - Why Study Music?
  - Music Education Around the World: Spotlight on a Global Issue
  - ISME advocacy program: a new partnership with Support Music Coalition[59]
- Advocacy: Children's Voices. This blog on the ISME website lists numerous comments about the positive impact of music study from children all over the world. (See Appendix Y.)
  - Have students recite these while an ensemble is playing or singing softly in the background.

- Display these comments, along with annotations from your own students, in a PowerPoint presentation before the concert begins.
- Include these comments, along with remarks from your own students, in an insert inside a concert program.
- Write a letter to policymakers and include an insert with statements from children in the local community and across the globe.[60]

Through the process of compiling the list of advocacy actions listed in this chapter, I reviewed multiple sources, books, and articles. Several recommendations were similar or exact duplicates, so some of the ideas and strategies were combined. In addition to the NAfME, NAMM and ISME websites, materials and recommendations in this chapter were compiled from the following individuals, articles, and documents. Log on to the accompanying website for this book to examine an even more comprehensive list of sources (www.oup.com/us/advocateformusic).

- Delgado, L. (2006). Advocacy tips, ideas, and strategies. Southwest Division of MENC Fall Division Meeting, Kansas City, MO. July 22–23, 2006.[61]
- Lane, M. (2014). Be proactive, not reactive! North by Northwest column, *Idaho Music Notes*, Winter 2014, 10.[62]
- Ouren, B. (2007). The MENC position statement on advocacy. *Interval* (Minnesota Music Educators Association), 39–40, 42.[63]
- Parsons, B. N. G. (2000). North Carolina coalition for music education. *North Carolina Music Educator*, Spring 2000, 10.[64]
- Schmidt, J. E. (2008). An uneasy alliance: Music education and public policy. *VOICE*, January 2008, 15–16.[65]
- Sletto, J. (2014). Thinking outside the box. *Teaching Music*, January 2014, 8.[66]
- Benham, J. L. (2011). *Music advocacy: Moving from survival to vision*. Rowman & Littlefield Education, New York, NY.[67]
  - Zeuch, K. (2013). Student times, extreme choral program makeover, advocacy edition. *Choral Journal, 53*(4), 73–74.[68]

SUMMARY

My goal is to help caring advocates build a toolbox of compelling reasons for music education. Advocates can share potential ramifications of a future society where children and adolescents have little or no access to fine arts education. We can all take action, help reform education, and make music for every child a reality instead of an outdated dream. Advocacy often reminds me of walking on the large dunes in White Sands, New Mexico. In March, after a spring rain, a person can easily cruise up those cream-colored slopes because the sand is moist and firm. Later in the summer, when the relentless sun takes over, the sand is quite slippery. For every three steps forward, you slide back two steps. Progress is possible, but the climbing is slow and laborious. That is what advocacy may feel like at times.

Music is difficult to quantify, because it connects the human spirit and creative mind. Once again, if our goal is to educate decision makers about the value of music education, then it is our job to build relationships with teachers, parents, legislators, administrators, school board members, and other community members. What is more, we need to search for ways to gain an understanding of others' interests and viewpoints. By looking at issues through another person's lens, people on both sides of the conversation can better relate to each other's concerns and challenges.

By using this book, music educators gain access to skills and strategies to respectfully share concerns and suggest solutions when meeting with decision makers. Also, the accompanying website supplies an extensive list of links to additional resources: advocacy organizations, websites, webinars, research articles, and blogs. Our world is changing at hyperspeed, and most of the time we just want to get through the day. All of the knowledge, experiences, and suggestions here are intended to help navigate our new reality and seize the new opportunities before us. This book supplied multiple answers to the question, "How do we advocate for music?" Earlier I shared the analogy of a recipe. Recipes can be modified and improved by adding new ingredients or taking away others. Take the ingredients (strategies and recommendations) that work for you and discard the others. Different advocacy strategies will resonate with different people.

Remember the old proverb that says, "Give a man a fish and he eats for a day; teach him to fish and he eats for a lifetime." NAMM CEO Mary Luehrsen shared that analogy of teaching people to fish with me in reference to advocacy. "We must build a network, whether it is a pond, a lake, or an ocean, so they have the tools to enable them to advocate for music."[69] Take the tools that propel you to act, because the message needs to reach numerous facets of society. Gear the message toward the intended recipients and address issues and concerns they care about. Sometimes the best advocacy strategy is to do something. Write that letter, send that email, make that phone call, or meet with decision makers—because in politics, the decision often belongs to those who show up.[70]

CALL TO ACTION

1. Three new advocacy actions I can incorporate at my upcoming performance/program are:
   a. _____.
   b. _____.
   c. _____.
2. The next time I talk to a group of parents I will ask them to:
   a. _____.
   b. _____.
   c. _____.

CHAPTER 5

When Should We Advocate for Music?

After covering the aspects of what, why, how, where, and to whom you should advocate, the next question is "When should we advocate for music?" This chapter outlines recommendations on when to use various strategies for optimum impact. We can develop a consistent, sequential progression of proactive actions and tactics to share the importance of music study in schools. And those actions have the potential to positively impact the future of our students, *if* we implement them. Proactive advocacy, rather than reactive measures, provides a better opportunity to educate decision makers and build relationships with all of the players involved: policymakers, administrators, school staff, teachers, parents, business, organizations, and so forth. By maintaining a keen understanding of the current status of music in schools, we stay informed and pay attention to activities and issues that have the potential to negatively impact students' access to music and the other arts in school.

CONSISTENT, RELENTLESS EDUCATION

In the 1990s, elected leaders and executive staff of the National Association for Music Education (NAfME)[1] agreed that music advocacy was a top priority for the association. That decision resulted in increased communication with legislators on Capital Hill in Washington, DC. The NAfME leadership and executive staff began providing additional advocacy training for the state leaders and their staff. A concerted effort to unify advocacy efforts and funds resulted in collaborations with other arts associations and professional associations.

Many advocacy actions can be implemented throughout the year. Others are more effective in a particular season. For example, making appointments to visit with congressional leaders may not be constructive if a teacher or parent travels to Washington, DC, during a scheduled recess. Working with the NAfME federated music education association (MEA) leadership and executive staff in your state can help ensure that your advocacy actions with a particular legislator support your state association's advocacy efforts, and that your actions are aligned with the legislative calendar.

Benham suggests that attending school board meetings is the best way to learn of an impending crisis or upcoming issues.[2] Consequently, the school board's schedule will affect the time frame for attending those meetings. Administrative decisions about program cuts are often determined in early fall, and the public may not become aware of these cuts until as late as January. School board meetings as late as June may still allow advocates to influence changes. Consider asking school board members to pass a resolution to support music education during March to coordinate with Music in Our Schools Month. An article entitled "MIOSM and Advocacy"[3] outlines specific details on how to implement this strategy.

Teachers who are overwhelmed by taking on yet another task can still contribute to advocacy processes by building and maintaining positive relationships with administrators, peer teachers, and parents. People who have more energy or time may want to scour the school calendar for joint events that might attract the attention of the local media. We teachers hope to share our craft and knowledge so that all students benefit. At the end of the day, we want our students to acquire knowledge, to learn how to learn, and to leave our classrooms each day confident that their time with us was worthwhile. Our students may one day be school board members, parents, coaches, business executives, and congressional leaders. Hopefully they will champion music education because of their time with us.

During my term as president of the Music Educators National Conference (MENC),[4] I chose the word *possibilities* for the title of my columns in *Teaching Music*[5] and *Music Educators Journal*.[6] Master teachers understand that our expectations exert a powerful influence on students' achievements.[7] We have a world of possibilities in front of us, and our success in advocating for music is only limited by our imaginations. It is possible to create a wave of influence even if each reader only implements one strategy from this guidebook. As an illustration, central Texans usually rejoice when it rains because of our seemingly endless drought. If we get too much rain, however, dry creek beds become rolling masses of water. A flood begins with a single raindrop, and advocacy can follow that same path.

This is an exciting time with abundant opportunities. As the pendulum of education guidelines and policies swings toward extreme testing and accountability, we can provide a unified voice. This book outlines tools to change the direction of music education. By using these tools, we can ensure that music study is maintained for the benefit of all students, not a select few. Everyone has the potential to influence policymakers and change how education is taught in our schools, as long as we honor and respect their view of the world.

We are educators first—and music teachers second. At the 2007 MENC Centennial Celebration and Congress, Mike Hyatt pointed out that education is more than the download of data from one brain to another.[8] If we truly intend to influence people with ideas and challenges that are new to them, then we know, as educators, that we begin teaching by starting with the issues, activities, and concepts they know and care about. Then we can guide them to open up their minds to new concepts and behaviors. Master teachers start with the familiar, and then they move forward to new information and skills. They build on the current knowledge base of their students. For example, we do not expect a choir to tackle a Bach chorale if the singers are struggling to consistently match pitches. It makes sense to me that we should approach advocacy from the same perspective. If our goal is to influence another's thinking about the value of study in music and the other arts, we need to be just as willing to learn about the other person's mindset before we set out to teach him or her about the benefits of music education. Insights gleaned from this interaction can help guide us as we elevate the conversation toward advocacy issues. Master educators pay attention to people and foster healthy relationships with the human beings in their classes and ensembles. They relentlessly search for ways to help their students learn. In *The Conductor as Leader*, Ramona Wis beautifully sums up what it is to be an educator: Educators invite, instruct, and inspire instead of coerce, drill, and punish.[9] Coercing, driving, and punishing hinder relationships with others. Strive to grasp a better understanding of the challenges others face. Look at the world through another's lens, and then help that person see music education's benefits through your eyes.

Eventually music can reside in the curriculum safe from constant budget cuts and reductions in class time. We are creating the musicians of the future, and we can change how legislation is interpreted. Be part of the force that catapults the message to encourage music making by all students.

SUMMARY

In Chapter 1, we explored the definition of music advocacy and discussed several reactive and proactive events to advocate for music education. Chapter 2 delved into several areas of research investigating the relationships between music study, student learning beyond the classroom, and brain development. The focus of Chapter 3 highlighted individuals, associations, and organizations with the potential to initiate effort toward a common goal of music advocacy. Chapter 4 delivered nearly 100 ideas and strategies to engage teachers and preservice teachers in advocacy actions.

In closing, Chapter 5 reminds us that the time for music advocacy is now. This book provides sufficient tools to equip music educators and preservice teachers to tailor advocacy strategies to meet their individual strengths and interests.[10] Just as music study expands across numerous genres, advocacy encompasses a wide range of activities and processes. Multiple ideas and strategies in the previous chapters can help every individual seize at least one tactic and implement it.

Finally, the appendices provide model documents, websites, strategies, materials, and lists of organizations that complete this resource guidebook. Review all of the items in the appendices and identify at least one idea or activity that resonates with your comfort level and passion to advocate for music. People are creatures of habit, and changing behaviors is a process. I often hear that habits are 1,000 times stronger than our desires. It is much easier to keep on doing the same thing over and over instead of conjuring up sufficient energy to initialize new behaviors and habits. With that in mind, map out a plan to do one new, unfamiliar advocacy action each month. Begin building advocacy muscles, because even incremental changes can make a big difference.

Earlier in the Preface, I used the analogy that this was a book of recipes for successful advocacy. At any time recipes can be changed and ingredients can be added or deleted. Take the recipes that fit your lifestyle and schedule. Solutions for finding innovative ways to support fine arts programs are abundant. This book supplies a number of means to advocate effectively and efficiently by delivering manageable strategies that match up with each individual's time, comfort level, energy, and financial resources to contribute to advocacy efforts.

Thank you for caring about kids. Caring is not enough though. Contributions are much like the ripples on a still pond when you skip a rock across the surface. One small contribution elicits another, then another, and then another. Once someone shares a gift with us, whether it is a thoughtful gesture, a new skill, or a physical object, we all benefit. We may be more inclined to pass on that positive energy to others. Our students, colleagues, families, school community, peers, and profession all reap the rewards. We do too. As we end this journey together, think about what the next step is. The gift of advocacy requires action. What will be your call to action? Start today and identify the strategies and ideas that resonate the most. Implement at least one strategy in the near future. Safeguard music education's rightful place in the schools to benefit all children and adolescents.

CALL TO ACTION

1. Three new actions or strategies I will implement this month are:
   a. _____.
   b. _____.
   c. _____.
2. At my next performance or program I will share these three pieces of information about music advocacy with the audience:
   a. _____.
   b. _____.
   c. _____.

Appendices

Most people are quite busy, and even those with the best of intentions may get sidetracked if an advocacy activity is too time intensive. The materials provided here can help teachers and preservice teachers focus their efforts through time-saving, efficient strategies. Consider this section of the book as your manual and resource guide for advocacy.

Chapter 4 provided a series of ideas and strategies for advocacy actions. These appendices furnish readers with immediate access to resources and materials to support those advocacy activities. Included are model letters and scripts for verbal and written communication to local, state, and national decision makers. In addition, there is an extensive list of websites that provide a multitude of advocacy resources. For even more recommendations, materials, and items to further the quest for successful music advocacy, visit this book's accompanying website (www.oup.com/us/advocateformusic).

Materials are presented under the following categories:

- Resources to Advocate With Education Institutions and the School Community
- Resources for Local/Community Advocacy
- Resources for State Advocacy
- Resources for National Advocacy
- Resources for International Advocacy
- Resources for Websites and Other Media

Documents may be copied exactly as they are presented. Consider modifying the language of the model letters to suit individual communication styles and situations; delivering 100 different letters that focus on the same issue or purpose has much more impact than delivering one identical letter from 100 different people. And adding personal anecdotes helps illustrate how music study makes a difference in students' lives in your community.

RESOURCES TO ADVOCATE WITH LOCAL EDUCATION INSTITUTIONS, LOCAL BUSINESSES, AND THE SCHOOL COMMUNITY

Appendix A—Advocacy Flyer, Parents

Figure A.1 shows the front page of an advocacy flyer for parents. Download it by logging on to http://www.nafme.org/take-action/advocacy-resources/how-to-advocacy-guides/.

Appendix B—Advocacy Inserts for Programs

Figure B.1 shows an insert that can be added to printed programs for performances. Download it by logging on to http://www.nafme.org/advocacy-inserts-for-concert-programs/. Include this PDF as an insert in your concert programs or other presentations.

Appendix C—Archived Webinars to Assist With Advocacy

This webinar, developed by the National Association for Music Education (NAfME) and shown in Figure C.1, outlines the process to participate in nationwide advocacy during Music in Our Schools Month.

Appendix D—Letter to Your Principal

The letter shown in Figure D.1 can be used exactly as it is written or modified to adapt to different situations. Consider including supportive materials, such as summaries of research articles, from other resources available in this book with the letter.

Appendix E—Advocacy Concert Speech

The speech shown in Figure E.1 can be used exactly as it is written or modified to adapt to specific audiences (and can be obtained from http://advocacy.nafme.org/files/2013/03/Advocacy-Concert-Speech.pdf). Hand out supplemental information, such as summaries of research articles, from other resources available in this book, or include the PDF in a concert program.

GRAB and GO ADVOCACY

Parents:
GET THE MESSAGE!

Parents are potentially the greatest source of support for your program. They see the benefits of your teaching when their kids come home full of chatter about music class. Parents are also quick to offer their time and energy to activities like fundraising and the logistics of concert planning and travel. They're also the best pool to draw upon for manpower in developing your advocacy efforts.

Messaging

Where to begin? Your parent coalition won't come together on its own. As with any group, members must be recruited, and that requires a compelling message.

Start by answering this question: What issues motivated them to take an interest in your advocacy initiative in the first place?

- Learning to play a musical instrument helps students build confidence. They take pride in their achievements, both individual and as members of an ensemble.
- Students who participate in music education programs see music as their "social glue," connecting them to one another and the wider world.
- On average, music students score higher on both the verbal and math portions of the SAT, helping them to get into good colleges and universities.
- Students who take music classes tend to have fewer drug and alcohol problems and fewer brushes with the law.
- Music education helps in the development of 21st-century skills that employers prize, including
  1) critical thinking and problem solving
  2) collaboration
  3) creativity
  4) initiative and self-direction
  5) leadership and responsibility

National Association *for* **Music Education**

Figure A.1 NAfME advocacy guide for parents.

So, how do you direct all the parental good will and enthusiasm to meet your advocacy goals?

- Send home a flyer with your students inviting their parents to an informal gathering to briefly discuss the advocacy team's mission. Let them know how valuable their contributions will be to their child's music education.
- Designate a "team leader" from among the volunteering parents once you have your team in place. It's your job to guide them, but let them take the initiative in researching the issues, collecting data, organizing events, scheduling meetings with district school boards and PTAs, etc.
- Work with your team to design a website for your advocacy campaign. Make sure it's updated regularly and frequently.
- Create a listserv so team members can communicate easily with one another.
- Have your team start a Facebook campaign to raise awareness of the benefits of music education for your students.
- Select a public relations contact for your team to engage the traditional media by publicizing every concert, meeting, and advocacy-related event.
- Meet with your team every few months to evaluate your efforts and assess whether the goals are being met. If they are, stick to your plan and keep in touch with your important contacts. If not, then decide what needs to be changed and keep at it. Patience, persistence (and good humor) are key in protecting a music education program.

The Bottom Line

Today's music educator is faced with a difficult choice: Either actively advocate on behalf of your program or run the risk of it falling victim to budget cuts when the time comes for school districts to make tough funding decisions. Protect your students' access to a comprehensive education that includes music education provided by exemplary music educators. Their futures may depend on it.

Questions?

Write to advocacy@nafme2.org or call (800) 336-3768.

© National Association for Music Education (www.nafme.org)

For today's students to succeed tomorrow, they need a comprehensive education that includes music education provided by exemplary music educators.

Figure A.1 (Continued)

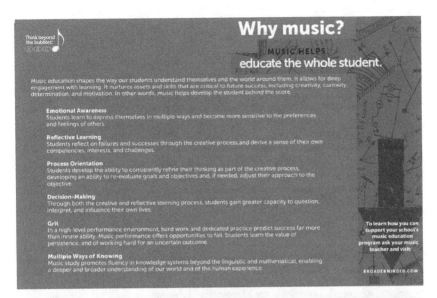

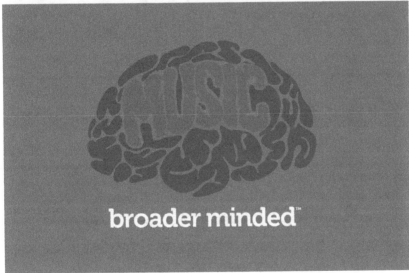

Figure B.1 NAfME "Why Music?" advocacy insert.
Copyright © 2014 NAfME/All Rights Reserved. Permission to use granted by NAfME.

Webinar: Celebrate Music in Our Schools Month!

Log on to the web-link provided below to find out how to participate in the NAfME Concert for Music in Our Schools Month each spring.

⟨http://www.nafme.org/take-action/webinar/⟩.

Figure C.1 NAfME webinar for Concert in Our Schools Month.
Copyright © 2014 NAfME/All Rights Reserved. Permission to use granted by NAfME.

Dear Principal [insert principal's name here],

U.S. Secretary of Education Arne Duncan penned a letter in August 2009 http://www.artsed-ucation.org/ArneDuncanArtsEdLetter.pdf in support of arts education. This letter can serve as a reminder to education administrators that Elementary and Secondary Education Act Title I funds may be used to fund music education in our schools. The Secretary writes, "At this time when you are making critical and far-reaching budget and program decisions for the upcoming school year, I write to bring to your attention the importance of the arts as a core academic subject and part of a complete education for all students. The Elementary and Secondary Education Act (ESEA) defines the arts as a core subject, and the arts play a significant role in children's development and learning process."

"Under ESEA, states and local school districts have the flexibility to support the arts. Title I, Part A of ESEA funds arts education to improve the achievement of disadvantaged students. Funds under Title II of ESEA can be used for professional development of arts teachers as well as for strategic partnerships with cultural, arts and other nonprofit organizations."

I hope you will pursue these funds for music education because, as you may already know, research shows that children who receive a comprehensive, sequential music education taught by exemplary music educators do better in overall school achievement, social development, success in society, and earning potential. Music helps prepare young minds to think creatively, learn how to work collaboratively, and to become disciplined, critical thinkers and problem solvers –skills needed in the 21st century economy.

Thank you for your consideration.

Sincerely,

[insert your name here]

(http://advocacy.nafme.org/files/2012/03/advocacy_letter_principal.pdf)

Figure D.1 Model letter to send to the school principal.
Copyright © 2014 NAfME/All Rights Reserved. Permission to use granted by NAfME.

"Welcome and thank you for attending our [e.g. winter/spring concert, senior night, showcase, etc].

While you enjoy the concert, please remember that in addition to the skills the students demonstrate, music education helps prepare young people to think creatively, learn how to work collaboratively, and to become disciplined, critical thinkers and problem solvers.

Research shows that children who receive a comprehensive, sequential music education taught by exemplary music educators do better in overall school achievement, social development, success in society, and earning potential.

Times are very tight fiscally, and music education is under threat in many places. If you recognize the value music education has for your child, your continued support of this program will help ensure that music remains an essential component of your child's education. After all, music and the arts are considered a "core" subject in the federal Elementary and Secondary Education Act.

Please let me know if you would like more information on how to become involved in supporting our music program. You can also contact NAfME, The National Association for Music Education (www.menc.org) with any questions about how you can support music in the schools.

Thank you for being here tonight, and I hope you will enjoy the hard work these students have put into making this program possible."

Figure E.1 NAfME advocacy speech to present at a performance.
Copyright © 2014 NAfME/All Rights Reserved. Permission to use granted by NAfME.

Appendix F—Grab and Go Advocacy: Flyer for Crisis Management

Figure F.1 shows the front page of an advocacy flyer to use in a crisis management situation. Download the entire document by logging on to http://www.nafme.org/take-action/advocacy-resources/how-to-advocacy-guides/.

Appendix G—Advocacy Flyer, Elementary School Principals

Figure G.1 shows the front page of an advocacy flyer for elementary school principals. Download the entire document by logging on to http://www.nafme.org/take-action/advocacy-resources/how-to-advocacy-guides/.

Appendix H—Advocacy Flyer, Secondary School Principals

Shown in Figure H.1 is the front page of an advocacy flyer for secondary school principals. Download the complete document by logging on to http://www.nafme.org/take-action/advocacy-resources/how-to-advocacy-guides/.

Appendix I—Advocacy Flyer, School Boards

Figure I.1 shows the front page of an advocacy flyer for school board members. Download the complete flyer by logging on to http://www.nafme.org/take-action/advocacy-resources/how-to-advocacy-guides/.

Appendix J—Archived Webinars and Web Links

Use the links provided in Figure J.1 to access archived webinars on a variety of topics to assist your advocacy actions in the school and local community.

Appendix K—Form Letter to the School Board or to Collect Signatures for an Alliance Coalition

The form letter shown in Figure K.1 can be modified to adapt to different school boards or to collect signatures. Consider printing off supportive materials, such as summaries of research articles, from other resources available in this book to include with this form letter.

GRAB and GO ADVOCACY
CRISIS MANAGEMENT
When Times Get Tough...

❶ Get the Facts Down—Develop a fact sheet. Make sure it's accurate and up-to-date. **Don't forget to include a couple of personal anecdotes about your program.** Legislators/administrators remember anecdotes better than facts. Too many statistics can be overwhelming.

❷ Know the Arguments—Be prepared to debate the issues and have ready answers when presented with uncomfortable questions. Testimony from a professional, knowledgeable educator will have a tremendous impact.

❸ Map the Power Structure—Determine which legislative or administrative bodies hold the power to improve your music program. Who are the most influential individuals? To whom are they responsible?

❹ Involve the Media—Invite your local newspaper's metro beat reporter to a school board meeting. They're always on the lookout for stories about students achieving great things. Social media, like NAfME Advocacy Groundswell, also help get the word out about your program.

❺ Follow Up—Write a letter of thanks following any meeting to reiterate your position. Be ready to provide more information if asked.

Want to know more?

- **Advocacy Central:** http://advocacy.nafme.org/page/advocacy-central

- **Benefits of the Study of Music:** http://advocacy.nafme.org/page/general-resources

- **Get the Message:** http://advocacy.nafme.org/page/how-to-advocacy-guides

Questions? Write to advocacy@nafme2.org or call (800) 336-3768
www.nafme.org/advocacy

National Association *for* Music Education   For today's students to succeed tomorrow, they need a comprehensive education that includes music taught by exemplary music educators.

Figure F.1 NAfME flyer to use when there is an advocacy crisis.
Copyright © 2014 NAfME/All Rights Reserved. Permission to use granted by NAfME.

Figure F.1 (Continued)

Figure G.1 NAfME advocacy flyer for elementary principals.
Copyright © 2014 NAfME/All Rights Reserved. Permission to use granted by NAfME.

Elementary School Principal as Advocate

Now that you've brought your principal on board, how can you best use him/her as an advocate for your program?

- Start by inviting your principal to observe you teaching your students. If he or she has a clear picture of the learning your students are engaged in, your principal will be a better advocate for your program.
- Invite your principal to open your concerts with a few remarks to the audience on the benefits of music study, which you provide.
- Ask your principal to speak on the music program's behalf at PTA and school board meetings. His/her words carry a lot of weight with these groups.
- Keep your principal up to date on all important issues concerning your program. His/her continued effective involvement is dependent upon you keeping him/her informed.
- Provide your principal with relevant research and hard data when he or she is pressured by their superiors to eliminate music education at your school.
- Create a collaborative environment in your advocacy efforts so that your principal feels like part of a team. Make sure he or she is intimately involved in any letter-writing or social media-based campaigns.
- Be sensitive to your principal's concerns. If you're both on the same page, it's much easier to work together to maintain the long-term health of your program.

The Bottom Line

Today's music educator is faced with a difficult choice. Either actively advocate on behalf of your own program or have it run the risk of falling victim to budget cuts when it comes time for school districts to make tough funding decisions. Protect your program and your students' access to a comprehensive education that includes music education provided by exemplary music educators. Their futures may depend on it.

Questions?

Write to advocacy@nafme2.org or call (800) 336-3768.

© National Association for Music Education (www.nafme.org)

For today's students to succeed tomorrow, they need a comprehensive education that includes music education provided by exemplary music educators.

Figure G.1 (Continued)

Secondary School Principals: GET THE MESSAGE!

Secondary School Principals are charged with one very important task: insuring that the nation's children are prepared to go off to college or university or out into the world ready to handle every challenge that awaits them.

Music education has a crucial role to play in achieving this goal, and support from the administration is essential to ensuring it keeps its place in the curriculum. With the principal as an ally, a music program stands a much better chance of surviving when cuts must be made to the school budget.

Messaging

What's the key to securing their support? They're under as much pressure to get results as you are. With more time and resources being devoted to science and math, they're often likely to look to other subjects if hard financial choices have to be made. The answer is a compelling message.

Start by answering this question. What issues are important to them and will serve as tools to recruit them as fellow advocates for your program?

- Schools with music programs have significantly higher graduation rates than those without programs (90.2% as compared to 72.9%).
- On average, music students score higher on both the verbal and math portions of the SAT, helping them to get into good colleges and universities.
- Students who take music classes tend to have fewer drug and alcohol problems and fewer brushes with the law.
- Music education helps in the development of 21st-century skills that employers prize, including
    1) critical thinking and problem solving
    2) collaboration
    3) creativity
    4) initiative and self-direction
    5) leadership and responsibility

National Association *for* Music Education

Figure H.1 NAfME advocacy flyer for secondary principals.

Secondary School Principal as Advocate

Now that you've brought your principal on board, how can you best utilize him/her as an advocate for your program?

- Invite your principal to observe you teaching your students. With a clear picture of the learning your students are engaged in, he or she will be a better advocate for your program.
- Invite your principal to open your concerts with a few remarks to the audience on the benefits of music study, which you provide.
- Ask your principal to speak on the program's behalf at PTA and school board meetings. His or her words carry a lot of weight with these groups.
- Keep your principal up to date on all important issues concerning your program. His or her continued effective involvement is dependent upon you keeping them informed.
- Provide your principal with relevant research and hard data any time they are pressured by their superiors to eliminate music education at your school.
- Create a collaborative environment in your advocacy efforts so that your principal feels like part of a team. Make sure he or she is intimately involved in any letter-writing or social media-based campaigns.
- Be sensitive to your principal's concerns. If you're both on the same page, it's much easier to work together to maintain the long term health of your program

The Bottom Line

Today's music educator is faced with a difficult choice. Either actively advocate on behalf of your own program or have it run the risk of falling victim to budget cuts when it comes time for school districts to make tough funding decisions. Protect your program and your students' access to a comprehensive education that includes music education provided by exemplary music educators. Their futures may depend on it.

Questions?

Write to advocacy@nafme2.org or call (800) 336-3768.

© National Association for Music Education (www.nafme.org)

For today's students to succeed tomorrow, they need a comprehensive education that includes music education provided by exemplary music educators.

Figure H.1 (Continued)

GRAB and GO ADVOCACY

School Board:
GET THE MESSAGE!

School boards are very important to maintaining the long-term health of a music program for one simple reason: they control the purse strings and have the last word on funding for schools in their districts. Convince them that music education is as important to the academic development of the nation's children as any other subject, and your students will never experience the loss of what is often the part of the school day they look forward to most.

Messaging

What's the key to securing their support? They're under a lot of pressure to make sure the books balance every fiscal year. With more time and resources being devoted to science and math, they're often likely to look to other subjects if hard financial choices have to be made. The answer is a compelling message.

Start by answering this question. What issues are important to them and will serve to persuade them that music education programs are an essential part of any curriculum?

- Schools with music programs have significantly higher attendance rates than those without programs (93.3% as compared to 84.9%).
- Schools with music programs have significantly higher graduation rates than those without programs (90.2% as compared to 72.9%).
- Students who take music classes tend to have fewer drug and alcohol problems and fewer brushes with the law.
- On average, music students score higher on both the verbal and math portions of the SAT, helping them to get into good colleges and universities.
- Music education helps in the development of 21st-century skills that employers prize, including
  1) critical thinking and problem solving
  2) collaboration
  3) creativity
  4) initiative and self-direction
  5) leadership and responsibility

National Association *for* Music Education

Figure I.1 NAfME advocacy flyer for members of the school board.

What's the best way to cultivate a good relationship with your local school board?

- Invite school board members to all your concerts. Make them feel welcome, and they will be much less inclined to cut your program.
- Schedule a performance by your students at all school board meetings. If board members see the results of your teaching for themselves, it will be much harder for them to make cuts to your program.
- Ask your principal to speak on the program's behalf at school board meetings. A principal's words can carry a lot of weight in these settings.
- Make sure you have relevant research and hard data on things like student test scores and budget figures on hand anytime you speak at school board meetings.
- And have your students' parents talk about the benefits of music education in their children's lives at school board meetings. A good anecdote is often more effective than a PowerPoint presentation full of statistical information.

The Bottom Line

Today's music educator is faced with a difficult choice. Either actively advocate on behalf of your own program or have it run the risk of falling victim to budget cuts when it comes time for school districts to make tough funding decisions. Protect your program and your students' access to a comprehensive education that includes music education provided by exemplary music educators. Their futures may depend on it.

Questions?

Write to advocacy@nafme2.org or call (800) 336-3768.

© National Association for Music Education (www.nafme.org)

For today's students to succeed tomorrow, they need a comprehensive education that includes music education provided by exemplary music educators.

Figure I.1 (Continued)

Advocacy at the School and Local Community

1. Webinar: Advocacy 101: Advocacy in the Community

This webinar focuses on ways to show support for music education in the community and how to inspire others to advocate on your behalf. Members from several states share about their local advocacy experiences, and share ideas to help spur your own local advocacy strategies.

(http://www.nafme.org/take-action/webinar/)

2. Webinar—The Council of Chief State School Officers (CCSSO)

The Council of Chief State School Officers is a nonpartisan, nationwide, nonprofit organization of public officials who head departments of elementary and secondary education in the states, the District of Columbia, the Department of Defense Education Activity, and five U. S. extra-state jurisdictions. CCSSO provides leadership, advocacy, and technical assistance on major education issues.

(http://www.nafme.org/take-action/advocacy-resources/state-resources/)

3. Webinar—Education Week

This link takes you to an on-line news source for K-12 leaders and policy experts.

(http://www.nafme.org/take-action/advocacy-resources/state-resources/)

Figure J.1 NAfME archived webinars for advocacy in the local school and community.
Archived Webinars, with Web links - Developed by NAfME

A document similar to the one provided below may be handed out at concerts and then collected at the end of the event. Then the collected signatures can be mailed or delivered to the president of the School Board.

Albuquerque Arts Alliance
Arts in Education Task Force

To _____ and Albuquerque Public School Board of Education Members:

I would like to express my support for arts education in our schools and specifically, expansion of arts education at the elementary level.

Please make the arts a priority in your educational plans for our students.

_____   _____

Signature   *Zip Code*

Figure K.1 Model document to collect signatures for music advocacy.

Appendix L—Letter to the Business Community

The letter shown in Figure L.1 (available from http://www.aep-arts.org/about-aep/partnering-organizations/our-partners/) was provided by Luis Delgado, director of fine arts, Albuquerque Public Schools.

Mr./Mrs._____
APS Board of Education
PO Box_____
Albuquerque, NM 87125
Date

Dr. Mr. _____:

My child attends _____ School, in of the schools in your district. I am writing to you both as a parent and as a business person to encourage you to expand the district's elementary Fine Arts program.

My daughter/son, _____, had an excellent experience with the art teacher who was assigned to her school. The work she brought home was colorful and enjoyed by the whole family. More important to us, however, was the confidence she gained at being able to express herself. This has carried over from her art to her writing as well.

From my professional perspective, my company has found it to be very important in recruiting new employees from out of state to be able to show that our school district values the arts. I have also found that employees in our company who have a liberal arts education and who have taken art, music or theater or dance courses themselves are the ones who are the most creative when it comes to problem-solving. They are also the ones who have the most respect for all types of diversity and the ones I can depend on to work well with their colleagues.

While I can appreciate the many difficult decisions that like ahead for you as a Board member, I urge you to make expansion of the elementary Fine Arts program one of your top priorities. From a business perspective, it is an investment for both our children as well as our community. And as a parent, I consider it to be an essential part of the education our children should receive.

Sincerely,

(Name, address, phone)

Figure L.1 Model letter to advocate for music with members of the business community.

Appendix M—Advocacy Checklist

Use the advocacy checklist in Figure M.1 as a model and develop your own that focuses on the unique needs of your school music programs and community support for the arts.

Every music teacher is encouraged to take the following ten basic steps to build and strengthen support for his or her program:

1. Take advantage of every possible opportunity to inform school officials, students' parents, and the public of the reasons why music should be included in the curriculum of every child.
2. Ensure that school officials, parents, and the public are aware of what your music program consists of and what its goals are; be certain that they know that your students are not merely singing and playing instruments but that they are acquiring valuable skills and knowledge in music that will enhance the quality of their lives for as long as they live.
3. Seek opportunities for your students to demonstrate their music skills and knowledge for parents and education decision-makers; student enthusiasm for music and proficiency in music are especially powerful tools in advocating for your program.
4. Develop regular contacts with the electronic and print media and with persons in the community who can influence education decision-makers.
5. Seek the support of other individuals and groups in the community that are interested in education and in the arts, and work with colleagues to develop coalitions at the local, province, state, and national levels to advocate on behalf of school music; broadly-based coalitions are much more effective than individuals or small groups in advocacy efforts.
6. Keep your message short and simple; length and complexity will tend to confuse and distract your audience.
7. Ensure that the music program in your school is of the highest possible quality.
8. Ensure that as many students as possible are involved in the music program in your school.
9. Undertake an advocacy activity at least once a week; do not wait until a crisis arises because then it may be too late.
10. Never assume that your program is so firmly established that no attention to advocacy is needed. (Paul Lehman, 8-26-04)

Figure M.1 Advocacy checklist.

Appendix N—Quotes to Support Music Education

Include the quotes shown in Figure N.1 (which can be obtained from http://advocacy.nafme.org/quotes/) in documents for distribution at school music programs and in letters to administrators.

Quotes to Support Music Education

"I must study politics and war that my sons may have liberty to study mathematics and philosophy. My sons ought to study mathematics and philosophy, geography, natural history, naval architecture, navigation, commerce, and agriculture, in order to give their children a right to study painting, poetry, musick, architecture, statuary, tapestry, and porcelaine."

—John Adams in letter to Abigail Adams, 12 May 1780

Figure N.1 Quotes to support music education.

"Music has the power of producing a certain effect on the moral character of the soul, and if it has the power to do this, it is clear that the young must be directed to music and must be educated in it."

—Aristotle, *Politics*

"Music washes away from the soul the dust of everyday life."

—Berthold Auerbach

"Music, of all the arts, stands in a special region, unlit by any star but its own, and utterly without meaning... except its own."

—Leonard Bernstein, *The Joy of Music*

"I grew up in the northside of Dublin in the beleaguered sixties and seventies–music meant everything to me ... Music is another language in which to express yourself. The feeling from music is liberating. It's the most liberating language of all."

—Bono ("Bill Clinton and Bono reveal how music changed their lives." Niall O'Dowd, Irish Central, May 7, 2010.)

"He who sings scares away his woes."

—Miguel de Cervantes

"I have said many times–if I hadn't been exposed to music as a child I don't think I would have been president."

—Bill Clinton ("Bill Clinton and Bono reveal how music changed their lives." Niall O'Dowd, Irish Central, May 7, 2010.)

"Music produces a kind of pleasure which human nature cannot do without."

—Confucius, *Book of Rites*

"If you would know if a people are well governed, and if its laws are good or bad, examine the music it practices."

— Confucius, *Analects*

"In the coming debate over ESEA reauthorization, I believe that arts education can help build the case for the importance of a well-rounded, content-rich curriculum in at least three ways. First, the arts significantly boost student achievement, reduce discipline problems, and increase the odds that students will go on to graduate from college. Second, arts education is essential to stimulating the creativity and innovation that will prove critical to young Americans competing in a global economy. And last, but not least, the arts are valuable for their own sake, and they empower students to create and appreciate aesthetic works."

—*The Well-Rounded Curriculum*, Secretary Arne Duncan's Remarks at the Arts Education Partnership National Forum, Omni Shoreham Hotel, Washington, DC, April 9, 2010

"I think I should have no other mortal wants, if I could always have plenty of music. It seems to infuse strength into my limbs and ideas into my brain. Life seems to go on without effort, when I am filled with music."

—George Eliot

"The only thing better than singing is more singing."

—Ella Fitzgerald

"To me, art in order to be truly great must, like the beauty of Nature, be universal in its appeal. It must be simple in its presentation and direct in its expression, like the language of Nature."

—Mahatma Gandhi, 1931, quoted in "Daily Hindu Wisdom" in the January 20, 2010
"When words leave off, music begins."

—Heinrich Heine

Figure N.1 (Continued)

"Music expresses that which cannot be said and on which it is impossible to be silent."
—Victor Hugo

"Some people think music education is a privilege, but I think it's essential to being human."
—Jewel

"The life of the arts, far from being an interruption, a distraction, in the life of the nation, is close to the center of a nation's purpose – and is a test to the quality of a nation's civilization."
—John F. Kennedy

"Music is to the mind as air is to the body."
—Plato

"Musical training is a more potent instrument than any other, because rhythm and harmony find their way into the inward places of the soul"
—*Plato*

"The language of music is common to all generations and nations; it is understood by everybody, since it is understood with the heart."
—Gioacchino Rossini, quoted in Zanolini, *Biografia di Gioacchino Rossini* (1875) *A Dictionary of Musical Quotations*. Ian Crofton, Donald Fraser, 1985

"There are two means of refuge from the miseries of life: music and cats."
—Albert Schweitzer

"Music has always had the ability to comfort and inspire."
—Pete Seeger

"Life isn't about finding yourself. Life is about creating yourself."
—George Bernard Shaw

"We need art as much as we need good works. You need it like food. You need it for inspiration, to keep going on the days that you're low. We need each other in that way."
—Meryl Streep

"The man who disparages music as a luxury and non-essential is doing the nation an injury. Music now, more than ever before, is a national need."
—Woodrow Wilson

Figure N.1 (Continued)

RESOURCES TO ADVOCATE AT THE STATE LEVEL

Appendix O—Archived Webinars and Web Links

Use the links provided in Figure O.1 to access archived webinars on a variety of topics to assist your advocacy actions at the state level.

Appendix P—The Non-Educator Performer in the Music Classroom (Position Statement)

Review the position statement in Figure P.1 (from http://www.nafme.org/about/position-statements/) addressing the issue of noneducator performers teaching music in the classroom. The position statement was developed by music educators in the field, NAfME leadership, and members of the NAfME staff.

Archived Webinars, with Web links - Developed by NAfME

Advocacy at the State Level

1. Webinar: Advocacy 201: Advocacy at the State Level

   In this archived webinar hear successful state level advocacy strategies and stories from NAfME MEA's and staff. With the possibility of less federal money going out to the states, this webinar helps make the case to our state elected officials that music education should be funded.

   http://www.nafme.org/take-action/webinar/

2. Webinar—Arts Education Partnership

   The Arts Education Partnership provides information and communication about current and emerging arts education policies, issues, and activities at the national, state, and local levels.

   http://www.nafme.org/take-action/advocacy-resources/state-resources/

3. Webinar—The Education Commission of the States

   This webinar provides non-partisan information about education policy to help state leaders develop education systems. It also includes state specific information and databases.

   http://www.nafme.org/take-action/advocacy-resources/state-resources/

Figure O.1 NAfME archived webinars for advocacy at the state level.

The Non-Educator Performer in the Music Classroom

The National Association for Music Education

Position

NAfME encourages professional collaborative relationships between music educators and visiting musicians and other presenters in the music classroom, with the understanding that these visiting musicians and presenters should make connections to the existing curriculum and work with educators to ensure student learning.

Concerns

The No Child Left Behind Law (NCLB) specifically states that all teachers must be "highly qualified" (meaning having demonstrable subject competence) and certified by the state in their subject area. However, individuals and groups from the community, such as parents, musicians, and music organizations, may be interested in presenting or sponsoring a presentation in a music classroom. Given that music instruction is often underfunded and understaffed, partnerships with arts and cultural organizations and services can be important resources for schools and positively affect student learning. Under no circumstances should a classroom presentation by a non-educator be a stopgap measure to supposedly integrate the arts or create an interdisciplinary curriculum. The mere presence of a musician or presenter does not automatically guarantee education, or even enrichment, in a classroom. In addition, a presenter who wants to teach but lacks state certification must work with the highly qualified teacher who is in charge of music instruction. The presenter's plan for the classroom must be approved first by the teacher who has the legal responsibility for the class. In terms of responsibility to students, presenters are not above accountability. They do not necessarily know more than the teacher, and it is important that students understand that a presenter's talent has been nurtured by learning, practice, commitment, and hard work. The teacher must design or approve the assessment, testing, or evaluative tools for the lessons the invited presenter offers.

Figure P.1 NAfME Position Statement: The Non-Educator Performer in the Music Classroom.

The Music Educator's Role

The music educator is a facilitator rather than a host for an event that includes a visiting musician. As a facilitator, the music educator should prepare both the students and the presenter in advance. As a facilitator, the music educator should have a role in, selecting the presenter, determining the focus, and planning the purpose of the visit, the activities in which students will be involved, and how the visit, presentation, and student learning will be evaluated. As the authority on teaching, the music educator can indicate that the presenter is expected to be prepared and professional, to maintain classroom control, to provide strategies and activities for engaging students' curiosity and interest, and to keep the goals for student learning clearly in mind. The music educator can also help the presenter focus on accountability and the top priority, which is the students' learning. After an event, the music educator can assist in assessment and evaluation, provide feedback to the presenter, and possibly recruit the presenter to participate in such issues as advocacy and funding for the arts.

Guidelines Before an event, the music educator can:

- Conduct planning sessions with the presenter so that the purpose, goals, and objectives of the event are clear and so that the event has a well-defined introduction, body, and conclusion. Included in this planning is telling the presenter about the pertinent school procedures and policies.
- Share teaching expertise. Find out about the pedagogical background and classroom experience of the presenter. Make sure that the presenter is able to establish positive relationships with the students, is aware of sound educational practices, such as accommodations for a variety of learning styles and intelligences, students' ages and backgrounds, and is prepared to ask students questions that require higher order thinking relevant to the music curriculum and the presentation.
- Discuss Standards. Determine how student time is spent during the event and how activities will align with content standards. Make sure that the program will elicit the desired measurable results.
- Plan for feedback. Help the presenter to plan ways to assess student learning. Prepare to provide the presenter with systematic feedback and assist in collection and review of data.
- Prepare students. Before the event, distribute materials giving students information about the presenter, the art form, and the music literature to be performed.

During an event, the music educator should:

- Emphasize to the students the importance of their participation and collaboration with the presenter.
- Help the presenter implement planned activities and deal with the unexpected.
- Help the presenter use clear, jargon-free language that the students can readily understand.

After an event, the music educator should:

- Document student learning.
- Work with the presenter to assess student progress.
- Use the assessment results to further improve the teaching plan.
- Encourage the presenter's commitment to student learning beyond the classroom.
- Use the assessment results to plan follow-up activities for the students.

Figure P.1 (Continued)

RESOURCES TO ADVOCATE AT THE NATIONAL LEVEL

Appendix Q—Letter to Arne Duncan, Secretary of Education

Use the letter to Arne Duncan, secretary of education, shown in Figure Q.1, as a model. Share this letter with parents and encourage them to write a letter to advocate for music education with national elected decision makers.

To:

Arne Duncan, Secretary of Education

U.S. House of Representatives

U.S. Senate

I believe that standards-based classroom music education should be accessible to every student in the United States. Music programs are key in helping students develop a broad range of skills and positive character traits, as well as find an inclusive school peer group. The majority of Americans not only strongly support music education but also say their personal experiences with music education prepared them for their future careers.

Despite this and music's designation as a core class, music has not been given the same priority as many other core subjects. Some music teachers are being improperly evaluated based on students' abilities in math and English, and all are regularly lumped into the category of "Other" in key Department of Education studies and left off of public lists of programs eligible to receive grants. (Music programs can receive this funding, according to a clarification letter released by the Secretary of Education.)

I urge you to respect music education by pushing for common-sense policy changes that recognize classroom music as its own vital discipline the way the majority of Americans already do. By opening up already available funding for quality music education programs and associated research, as well as clarifying language on best practices, we can create an environment that allows music to help our students succeed.

Sincerely,

[Your name]

Figure Q.1 NAfME letter to Arne Duncan, secretary of education.

Appendix R—Broader Minded: Think Beyond the Bubbles

Log on to the website link provided in Figures R.1A and R.1B and explore the multifaceted strategies provided by NAfME's Broader Minded Campaign, which advocates to keep music education in our schools.

Appendix S—Archived Webinars and Web Links

Use the links provided in Figure S.1 to access archived webinars on a variety of topics to assist your advocacy actions with national elected leadership.

Appendix T—Music Education Policy Roundtable Advocacy Documents for Federal Legislation Requests

Members of the Music Education Policy Roundtable developed the items shown in Figure T.1 to assist in music advocacy. Log on to the following website: http://www.nafme.org/take-action/music-education-policy-roundtable/.

Thinking Beyond the Bubbles: Developing a New, Broader Minded Argument for Music Education

by Christopher Woodside, *NAfME Assistant Executive Director, Center for Advocacy and Public Affairs*

All things considered, I think of myself as a pretty lucky individual. I am employed by a solid organization working for a wonderful cause, advocating for music education, and compared with most lobbyists, I sleep just fine at night. Now, granted, music can be a tough issue to "sell" up on Capitol Hill during lean economic times (see: NOW), but it is also rare to find anyone willing to go so far as to publicly disparage its value. Pretty much everyone you meet either already understands, or can eventually be convinced that providing students with access to high-quality music programs is a no brainer. Most importantly, music education advocates know exactly what we believe in and how to make an effective case for our issue, so it is simply a matter of doing the best that we can under sometimes impossibly challenging circumstances, right?

As a community of advocates, we make our arguments about the academic impact that access to music can have on other subjects like math and reading, talk about how schools with programs appear to maintain better graduation rates, testify that music is proven to light up the brains of both infants and the infirm, and remind principals that students are likely to perform better on their Common Core bubble exams, if only they would please, just pretty please, maintain and support those poor, beleaguered little music programs. This strategy has always been good enough for our little sliver of the education universe, so there is really no need to go reinventing the wheel.

Or is there?

All together, I have been working with music educators and music education advocates for almost a decade now. While my formal education and background is in public policy, my personal and family history is steeped in music and the arts, and over my most formative years, through a variety of experiences, I have gained a rather profound understanding of how important a role music can play in the lives of people of all ages. Over the entirety of the time period that I have been a part of promoting the music education cause, however, a connection that I have never personally succeeded in making is how our most central music advocacy arguments reflect the inherent "specialness" of music education and what it has to offer to classroom students. I would always prefer to let them speak for themselves, but I feel confident that my colleagues who constitute the remainder of the National Association for Music Education's expert advocacy staff, feel similarly about this issue.

For years, the problem has loomed over all of us involved in music advocacy, like a black storm cloud waiting to erupt. Here at the National Association for Music Education, we have gone about our business, wholly committed to teaching music educators to make the case for their discipline based on a tried-and-true advocacy formula, and, in doing so, have succeeded in making substantial progress toward indoctrinating the masses and ginning up enthusiasm in the public conscience for protecting classroom music. All the while, however, there has been a nagging feeling that something is amiss.

Visit www.broaderminded.com
National Association for Music Education

Figure R.1A NAfME campaign: Thinking Beyond the Bubbles: Developing a New, Broader Minded Argument for Music Education.

Over the years, advocacy trainers and trainees have spent a great deal of time and energy focusing on arguments that are well-intentioned, and, in some cases, even quite effective, but which often are not central to the unique benefits of music education. What this process has given rise to is a generation of music education advocates delivering a message that has been molded and shaped to acquiesce to the political and economic priorities of countless outside influences, but which, in some signifiant part, neglects the musical forest (of which we all hold so dear) for the trees. Essentially, the crux of the impasse at which we now find ourselves as a music education family, is this: we have not been making the case for our discipline based primarily on arguments that are about "music for music's sake." Hence, it is my opinion that much of the feeling of satisfaction we have thus far derived from the current strategy is a direct result of kowtowing to exterior forces.

Once acknowledged, addressing this problem is not something that can be accomplished overnight. In the last two years, the National Association for Music Education has devoted a great deal of time and resources to collecting intelligence on the manner in which our members have been conducting their advocacy work, and to analyzing the feedback for clues. As a result of this deeply extensive information collection undertaking (which has consisted of meeting with music educators from all across the country), we, as an institution, have gained a much more thorough understanding of what is working in music advocacy, and what is not.

Upon reaching the conclusion of this process, with access to all of the knowledge that we have since acquired, the National Association for Music Education can now say with absolute certainty: there is a better way.

Just to be clear, it is not that talking about music's impact on bubble tests and brain development is useless or irrelevant. Both of these examples represent wonderful potential benefits of exposure to a sequential, standards-based music education program. They absolutely should not, however, constitute the foundational argument that music advocates rely upon for the continued existence of programs. And why not? Because each and every time that we, as a music education community, profess that, most importantly, students should have access to music so that their brains become better wired to solve math equations, we provide ammunition to the camp of "education experts" who would presume to proclaim that music is an interchangeable, or (even worse), expendable, classroom experience.

As we all know, in reality, access to many different kinds of subjects and activities can be the catalyst for students achieving better math and reading scores, schools mustering better graduation rates, or even kids staying off of drugs. So, as music advocates, we must then ask ourselves, do we really want to hang our collective hat on making the case that music education is the be-all end-all when it comes to providing students with access to these benefits? If we do, then I'm not exactly sure where that leaves us when the table tennis and flag football folks come calling, or the student government association, or even the chess club, but it's probably not anywhere particularly good.

Music education, for its own sake, is indispensable to providing students with a rich and comprehensive learning experience; it is a "core" tenet of the school day. In order for our advocacy efforts to be truly successful, we must begin to talk about it in that way. As the leader in the music education advocacy space, the National Association for Music Education has developed a strategy for doing so, and soon, we hope that all music educators will be speaking this empowering new advocacy language.

Visit www.broaderminded.com
National Association for Music Education

Figure R.1A (Continued)

As we begin to explore the implications of what such a profound shift in our collective advocacy attitude will require, a note about accountability is in order. Over the years, many music educators have approached us to express their hesitancy at advocating for music for music's sake, based on a fear of not being taken seriously by principals and/or administrators in the current assessment-heavy climate. Rest assured, the National Association for Music Education takes music education assessment incredibly seriously.

Right now, brilliant minds within the Association are hard at work (along with their peers in the arts disciplines) on the next iteration of the National Standards for Arts Education. Further, a quick trip to NAfME.com is all that is required to familiarize oneself with the tireless efforts that have been undertaken by the Association in order to tackle the need to institute systems of equitable teacher evaluation across our field. Position papers, legislative language, advocacy guides, and workbooks are all available to the resourceful music educator. Similarly, all music advocates should be aware that this fundamental rethinking of our advocacy direction continues to take into consideration and speak directly to the accountability issue.

We know quite well that music educators are anything but shy about being assessed. In our experience, they accept it as an invaluable element of the music teaching process, and as a fundamental component of the profession. Personally, I am, in fact, yet to meet a music educator who did not fully embrace the idea of appropriate and fair assessment.

Bearing all of that in mind, at the National Association for Music Education, we do not detach the idea of advocating based upon music's inherent benefits from the need to assess a teacher's performance in the classroom. What we cannot support, however, and what our new advocacy initiative does not accept, is the premise that music educators should be evaluated based upon criteria that is not germane to their subject of expertise.

Music is not a "supplemental" discipline; it does not exist within the curriculum simply to benefit the teaching of other core subjects. After all, music educators have been practicing refined methodologies of assessment for centuries on end — evaluation is hardly a revolutionary concept in our field. As such, it is our belief that, quite frankly, our colleagues charged with developing accountability systems across the other core disciplines could stand to learn a thing or two about best practices in assessment from the music education community, rather than the other way around.

Once again, our new advocacy philosophy will not shy away from accountability. But at the National Association for Music Education, we do not believe in accountability to testing companies; we believe in accountability to students — period. That, in essence, is what 'Broader Minded: Think Beyond the Bubbles' is all about.

To truly begin talking about music as core, what we require as a field is a more complete, properly prioritized argument for music education. An argument that, yes, encapsulates everything that we have always touted about the virtues of exposure to music, from academic achievement, to brain development, to gap filling prophecies, but which also goes beyond the bubbles of standardized testing and the Common Core, and prioritizes music for music's sake — first and foremost. What we have long needed, is a Broader Minded argument for music education. *Flash forward to today...*

With tremendous excitement, we can now officially announce that, over the course of the next few weeks, the National Association for Music Education will begin the process of reimagining the manner in

Visit www.broaderminded.com
National Association for Music Education

Figure R.1A (Continued)

which we teach and conduct music education advocacy. In short order, we plan to set out upon a mission to return our advocacy efforts to their roots, back to an undisputed focus upon the inherent benefits of classroom music. Most importantly, through this incredibly uplifting and long overdue initiative, we will ALL, as a music education family, become comfortable again with talking about the benefits of music for music's sake.

As previously mentioned, this new Broader Minded identity for music education advocacy will demand a fundamental rethinking of how we go about conducting our work, and what we prioritize when making our case. While environmental factors such as national policy discussions, state and local-level budget negotiations and testing carrots and sticks will, of course, always influence the manner in which we shape our arguments, they will no longer serve as the single determinant factor. Certainly, we will continue to tailor our advocacy efforts to the priorities and needs of varying audiences and circumstances, but we will cease considering ourselves beholden to them. From this point forward, advocating for music education will mean shining the brightest spotlight upon the intrinsic values that music represents, with all other arguments serving in a still important, yet largely supplemental role.

Making this transition, from a community of advocates influenced by outside forces, to becoming a bottom-up, grassroots-fed "movement" of music education champions with our own unique sales pitch, will fundamentally alter the playing field. It will legitimize our efforts in the eyes of both supporters and detractors — permanently. So, how do we go about doing it?

Broken down into chunks, and then pieced back together as one, the Broader Minded argument for music education holds the answer. In addition to the aforementioned benefits, and, of course, the always important 21st Century Skills, which apply so meaningfully to our discipline (creativity, collaboration, confidence, critical thinking), thinking beyond the bubbles requires focusing upon the innate "specialness" of the music value proposition. The unique benefits of music education, look like this:

- Emotional Awareness: Students learn to express themselves in multiple ways and become more sensitive to the preferences and feelings of others.

- Reflective Learning: Students reflect on failures and successes through the creative process, and derive a sense of their own competencies, interests and challenges.

- Process Orientation: Students develop the ability to consistently refine their thinking as part of the creative process, developing an ability to reevaluate goals and objectives, and, if needed, adjust their approach to the objective.

- Agency: Through both the creative and reflective learning process, students gain greater capacity to question, interpret, and influence their own lives.

- Grit: In a high-level performance environment, hard work and dedicated practice predicts success far more than innate ability. Music performance offers opportunities to fail. Students learn the value of persistence, and of working hard for an uncertain outcome.

- Multiple Ways of Knowing: Music study promotes fluency in knowledge systems beyond the linguistic and mathematical, enabling a deeper and broader understanding of our world and of the human experience.

Visit www.broaderminded.com
National Association for Music Education

Figure R.1A (Continued)

By prioritizing the value proposition of intrinsic MUSIC benefits, and marrying this new, all-encompassing approach to advocacy with the countless amazing stories that we know music educators and others touched by music can share about the profound impact of access to programs, we can successfully employ the Broader Minded argument for music education, to great results.

At this point, I hope that you are all as excited about this new approach to music education advocacy as we are at the National Association for Music Education. With regard to this campaign and all of our advocacy initiatives, it is always our goal to provide music educators with the tools necessary to succeed both inside the classroom and out.

To that end, you may now be wondering, "How do I get started making the Broader Minded case for music education?" Well, I have good news to report — beginning February 18th, you can visit our new BroaderMinded.com website for all of your music advocacy needs. At that time, try your hand at the new 'Broader Minded Builder' landing page (make your case), order brochures to help advocate for your program, or purchase cheerful new Broader Minded gear — it will all be available online.

Should you have questions about the Association's new Broader Minded approach to music education advocacy, please feel free to contact me directly at chrisw@nafme.org, or reach out to Shannon Kelly at shannonk@nafme.org. We are here to support the music education community's advocacy work and are always more than happy to help. Thank you so much for all that you do; keep advocating for music and orchestrating success for students all across America, each and every day!

Visit www.broaderminded.com
National Association for Music Education

Figure R.1A (Continued)

broader minded

THINK BEYOND THE BUBBLES:

- In an age where teachers are forced to focus solely on narrowly construed measures of educational success (i.e. standardized tests and other quantifiable achievement scores), music education offers a unique opportunity to engage deeply with students' creativity, curiosity, and motivations.
- Studies have shown positive links between engagement with music and academic achievement. While important, these data are still a small part of the big picture. Music helps develop the student behind the score—students who are curious, motivated, engaged, and confident in their ability to succeed in our society.

BROADER-MINDED ARGUMENTS FOR MUSIC EDUCATION:

- Music students have a unique opportunity to receive immediate feedback and to reflect on their progress, make needed adjustments, and improve based on their own observations of their performance.
- Students learn the value of discipline, determination, and "grit"—achieving goals in the face of obstacles.
- Students get the chance to fail, and try again. They gain confidence and self-understanding, and learn to manage better their emotions and decision-making processes.
- Students get the chance to develop a greater emotional awareness through music, particularly during collaboration, and to consider the thoughts and feelings of others.
- Students get the chance to develop a tolerance for process. They refine their thinking as part of the creative process; they gain the ability to re-evaluate goals and adjust approaches to an objective.

CONCLUSIONS:

- We believe that music education is invaluable in developing successful students. Music shapes the way our students understand themselves and the world around them. It allows for deep engagement with learning. It nurtures assets and skills that are critical to future success.
- Because of the special qualities and skills it helps to instill, we believe that music is essential to a superior 21st-century education.
- This is the broader-minded argument for music education. It's about bringing balance back to the curriculum, and the ways in which music offers opportunities to excel. We're bringing the focus back to the student, not the score.

VISIT www.broaderminded.com

NATIONAL ASSOCIATION FOR MUSIC EDUCATION

Figure R.1B NAfME Broader Minded media talking points.

Archived Webinars, with Web links - Developed by NAfME

Advocacy at the National Level

1. Webinar: Hill Day 2014, How to Schedule a Meeting with Your Legislator

   This archived webinar covers all of the aspects necessary for scheduling a meeting with a legislator.

   http://www.nafme.org/take-action/webinar/

2. Webinar - Arts Education Partnership

   Research on arts education research is provided, with reports on the status of arts education in a number of states.

   http://www.nafme.org/take-action/advocacy-resources/state-resources/

3. Webinar: Back to School NAfME Advocacy

   To kick off a new school year, this webinar provided updates on progress in national and state advocacy work; and new advocacy initiatives or the coming year.

   http://www.nafme.org/take-action/webinar/

4. Webinar: NAfME Hill Day 2013

   This archived webinar outlined all of the materials, scheduling, and transportation issues for setting up a meeting with legislators.

   http://www.nafme.org/take-action/webinar/

5. Webinar: The Post-Election Landscape and Music Education

   Guest speaker Joel Packer, Executive Director of the Committee for Education Funding, gives an overview of the election results and what it means for education; more specifically, what it means for non-STEM subjects including music and the arts.

   http://www.nafme.org/take-action/webinar/

6. Webinar—Arts Education Partnership

   This discusses the collective voice of the nation's governors and one of Washington, D. C.'s most respected public policy organizations. Its members are the governors of the 50 states, three territories and two commonwealths.

   http://www.nafme.org/take-action/advocacy-resources/state-resources/

7. Webinar: Teacher Evaluation and Assessment in an Era of Education Reform

   Many states are implementing new teacher evaluation policies based in part on the accountability mandates from Race to the Top grants and ESEA (formerly NCLB) waivers. Learn more about this policy trend and what teachers in some states are doing to work with the new processes.

   http://www.nafme.org/take-action/webinar/

8. Webinar: Reinvesting in Arts Education: Winning America's Future Through Creative Schools

   Get an insider's look at Reinvesting in Arts Education, a report released by the President's Committee on the Arts and Humanities (pcah.gov). The research clearly shows the effect of arts education on student academic achievement and creativity. Rachel Goslins, Executive Director of PCAH, shares more about the study, and answers questions in a unique learning and discussion opportunity.

   http://www.nafme.org/take-action/webinar/

9. Watch a SupportMusic Coalition Teleconference and Webcast Recorded "LIVE" from the NAMM Show. Hear guest moderator Mike Blakeslee, Sr. Deputy Executive Director, NAfME as he leads an accomplished panel of music educators in a discussion on "Building and Engaging Support for Music and Arts Education".

   http://official-isme.blogspot.com/2012/01/10-why-study-music.html

Figure S.1 NAfME archived webinars for advocacy at the national level.

Music Education Policy Roundtable's legislative priorities for the 2015 reauthorization of ESEA:

1. **STRENGTHENED STATUS:** In order to strengthen the importance of music education in the law, for purposes of both garnering state-level funding and other forms of support, we ask that Congress maintain the core academic subject section in any reauthorization of the Elementary and Secondary Education Act.
2. **INCREASED ACCESSIBILITY:** In order to ensure that even the most disadvantaged of students have access to high quality music education programs, no matter their personal circumstance or background, we ask that Congress strengthen language throughout any reauthorization of the Elementary and Secondary Education Act, so as to increase clarity as to the availability of such resources, for use in this regard.
3. **EQUITABLE TEACHER EVALUATION:** In order to ensure that music educators are always evaluated by qualified individuals utilizing reliable measures germane to their discipline of study, and to make certain that ultimate accountability for all such measures is directly attributable to music teachers themselves, we ask that Congress offer language in any reauthorization of the Elementary and Secondary Education Act, recommending the institutionalizing of this practice.
4. **BALANCED ACCOUNTABILITY:** In order to ensure that, in making school district accountability determinations, "well-rounded" factors, such as achievement in music, are considered, in addition to state assessment results in reading/language arts and mathematics, we ask that Congress recognize the reliability of such multiple measures of performance, in developing corresponding State plans, in any reauthorization of the Elementary and Secondary Education Act.
5. **ENHANCED TEACHER PREPARATION:** In order to ensure that all federal granting opportunities for purposes of preparing, training, and recruiting high quality teachers and principals include a measure of consideration as to the importance of high quality music and arts education delivery abilities, we ask that Congress insert further clarifying language in any reauthorization of the Elementary and Secondary Education Act.

(http://www.nafme.org/standing-up-for-music-teachers-on-capitol-hill/)

Figure T.1 NAfME Music Education Policy Roundtable's legislative priorities for the 2015 reauthorization of Elementary and Secondary Education Act of 1965, Public Law 101–110 (ESEA).

Appendix U—"Vision 2020" Housewright Declaration

This document, shown in Figure U.1, is a summation of the agreements made at the Housewright Symposium on the Future of Music Education, held in Tallahassee, Florida, September 23–26, 1999.

Whenever and wherever humans have existed music has existed also. Since music occurs only when people choose to create and share it, and since they always have done so and no doubt always will, music clearly must have important value for people.

Music makes a difference in people's lives. It exalts the human spirit; it enhances the quality of life. Indeed, meaningful music activity should be experienced throughout one's life toward the goal of continuing involvement.

Music is a basic way of knowing and doing because of its own nature and because of the relationship of that nature to the human condition, including mind, body, and feeling. It is worth studying because it represents a basic mode of thought and action, and because in itself, it is one of the primary ways human beings create and share meanings. It must be studied fully to access this richness.

Figure U.1 "Vision 2020" Housewright Declaration.

Societal and technological changes will have an enormous impact for the future of music education. Changing demographics and increased technological advancements are inexorable and will have profound influences on the ways that music is experienced for both students and teachers.

Music educators must build on the strengths of current practice to take responsibility for charting the future of music education to insure that the best of the Western art tradition and other musical traditions are transmitted to future generations.

We agree on the following:

1. All persons, regardless of age, cultural heritage, ability, venue, or financial circumstance deserve to participate fully in the best music experiences possible.
2. The integrity of music study must be preserved. Music educators must lead the development of meaningful music instruction and experience.
3. Time must be allotted for formal music study at all levels of instruction such that a comprehensive, sequential and standards based program of music instruction is made available.
4. All music has a place in the curriculum. Not only does the Western art tradition need to be preserved and disseminated, music educators also need to be aware of other music that people experience and be able to integrate it into classroom music instruction.
5. Music educators need to be proficient and knowledgeable concerning technological changes and advancements and be prepared to use all appropriate tools in advancing music study while recognizing the importance of people coming together to make and share music.
6. Music educators should involve the music industry, other agencies, individuals, and music institutions in improving the quality and quantity of music instruction. This should start within each local community by defining the appropriate role of these resources in teaching and learning.
7. The currently defined role of the music educator will expand as settings for music instruction proliferate. Professional music educators must provide a leadership role in coordinating music activities beyond the school setting to insure formal and informal curricular integration.
8. Recruiting prospective music teachers is a responsibility of many, including music educators. Potential teachers need to be drawn from diverse backgrounds, identified early, led to develop both teaching and musical abilities, and sustained through ongoing professional development. Also, alternative licensing should be explored in order to expand the number and variety of teachers available to those seeking music instruction.
9. Continuing research addressing all aspects of music activity needs to be supported including intellectual, emotional, and physical responses to music. Ancillary social results of music study also need exploration as well as specific studies to increase meaningful music listening.
10. Music making is an essential way in which learners come to know and understand music and music traditions. Music making should be broadly interpreted to be performing, composing, improvising, listening, and interpreting music notation.
11. Music educators must join with others in providing opportunities for meaningful music instruction for all people beginning at the earliest possible age and continuing throughout life.
12. Music educators must identify the barriers that impede the full actualization of any of the above and work to overcome them.

NOTE: *This document is a summation of the agreements made at the Housewright Symposium on the Future of Music Education, held in Tallahassee, Florida, September 23-26, 1999.*

http://musiced.nafme.org/resources/vision-2020-housewright-declaration/

Figure U.1 (Continued)

CONTENTS

Open Letter from *Mary Luerhsen*, International Foundation for Music Research Foreward by *Kristen Madsen*, The Grammy Foundation

September 1, 2005

International Foundation
for Music Research

Dear Friends:

Music education is one of the cornerstones of a well-rounded and quality education. For much of the 20th century, children schooled in U.S. public schools had access to quality, sequential music education. It was integral to an education that grounded students in skills for productive work and lives.

In the last decades of the 20th century, music education came under threat and was marginalized in the school curriculum. This threat was realized in the elimination of thousands of programs and substantial cutbacks of qualified and certified music educators.

It is believed that music education is a subject with intrinsic cultural and artistic value and a skill-based activity that nurtures developmental and cognitive aspects of every child. However, only recently have the benefits of active participation in music been quantified through scientific research. Also only recently, new information provided by this research has informed the education policy debate.

This growing body of research data has helped define music education's benefits as part of a complete education and has provided baseline arguments to move music education back into the core curriculum. The latter remains a long-term goal for genuine renewed access to music education for every child in every school. In the short term, these research-based arguments have helped restore programs, stemmed the tide of some program cut backs and underpinned arguments for music and art education in the language of education policy and legislation.

The "Sounds of Learning" initiative seeks to expand the body of research about music education's intrinsic and extrinsic benefits. It is hoped that the initiative will yield new knowledge for the field of music education. Ultimately, we look to these research outcomes along with other research to fuel ongoing policy debates about what constitutes a meaningful and quality education for our nation's children.

The Foundation wishes to express its deepest appreciation to the skilled and inspiring Steering Committee of the "Sounds of Learning" initiative and to our partnering supporters, the Fund for Improvement of Education at the U.S. Department of Education and the Grammy Foundation. It also expresses deep gratitude to our founding and on- going affiliate, NAMM, the International Music Products Association.

Sincerely,

Mary Luehrsen
Executive Director

International
Foundation for Music

Research
5790 Armada Drive,
Suite 200
Carlsbad, CA USA, 92008
IFMR@music-research.org
www.music-research.org
phone: 760.438.5530
fax: 760.438.7327

FOREWARD

Kristen Madsen
Grammy Foundation

The mission of the GRAMMY Foundation is to cultivate an awareness, appreciation and advancement of the impact of music on American culture. In our efforts to achieve that objective, the Foundation has developed a wide range of music education and advocacy programs. Historically, the importance these programs—and music education programs nationwide—has been asserted in large part through passionately articulated anecdotal evidence of the positive impact of music education. The Sounds of Learning Project endeavors to sponsor and collect statistically significant evidence on the perceived positive benefits of music education. Utilizing a consistent and systematic evaluation process to reveal actual causes and links from the impact of music education, an expanded repository of research will be available on the subject.

Developing a blueprint of all the results that derive from music education will not only validate effective music instruction already established and inspire the creation of innovative curricula, but also inform the dialogue with policy makers and funding providers of education programs nationwide. The GRAMMY Foundation is proud to be a partner with the International Foundation for Music Research in funding the Sounds of Learning project.

1.
THE SOUNDS OF LEARNING PROJECT

Donald A. Hodges

The University of North Carolina at Greensboro

Sounds of Learning: The Impact of Music Education is a major research initiative designed to examine the roles of music education in the lives of school-age children and to expand the understanding of music's role in a quality education. Sounds of Learning (SoL) is an initiative of the International Foundation for Music Research (IFMR), with additional funding provided by the Fund for Improvement of Education from the U.S. Department of Education and the Grammy Foundation. A major goal of the project is to examine music education's influence on:

(a) Achievement and success in school,
(b) All aspects of a child's growth and development,
(c) The uses and functions of music in daily life, and
(d) Home, school, and community environments.

A unique feature of this project is that significant funding is available to support research designed to advance our understanding of the impact of music education.

SoL is guided by the following Steering Committee:

> Edward P. Asmus, Professor of Music Education and Associate Dean, University of Miami Frost School of Music
> Paul A. Haack, Professor of Music Education, University of Minnesota School of Music
> Donald A. Hodges, Covington Distinguished Professor of Music Education; Director, Music Research Institute, University of North Carolina at Greensboro School of Music
> Mary Luehrsen, Executive Director, International Foundation for Music Research Kristen Madsen, Senior Vice President, The Grammy Foundation
> Debra S. O'Connell, Posdoctoral Fellow, University of North Carolina at Greensboro School of Music
> Patricia E. Sink, Graduate Advisor for Music Education, University of North Carolina at Greensboro School of Music
> David J. Teachout, Chair, Division of Music Education, University of North Carolina at Greensboro School of Music

Biographical descriptions of Steering Committee members can be found in Appendix A.

During an initial organizational meeting, the Steering Committee organized the Sounds of Learning project into three phases, with the following timeline:

Phase 1
—2005—
February 11-13: initial Steering Committee meeting
March 3: Phase 1 Request for Proposals (RFPs) announced
May 1: announcement of research award recipients
July 1: *SoL Status Report* drafts due
August 1-3: second Steering Committee meeting
September 1: release of first draft *SoL Status Report* and Database; dissemination to selected reviewers for review and commentary
Phase 2
September 1: Phase 2 RFPs announced
October 1: deadline for reviewers to return critiques
November 1: deadline for submission of Phase 2 RFP proposals
December 3-4: third Steering Committee meeting
December 5: announcement of Phase 2 RFP recipients; release of second draft of *SoL Status Report* soon thereafter
—2006—
January 3: Final Reports of Phase 1 research projects due
Feb. 18-19: Steering Com. meeting and Research Awards Conference with Phase 1 & 2 RFP recipients
Phase 3
September 1: Phase 3 RFPs announced
December 1: Final Report of Phase 2 research projects due
—2007—
February: publish revised *SoL Status Report*, including a compendium of all funded research
February: Sounds of Learning national summit, Washington, D.C.

PHASE 1

Phase 1 included the previously mentioned Steering Committee meeting, announcement and contracting for initial research proposals, and release of the *SoL Status Report* and Database.

Phase 1: Request for Proposals

Three Requests for Proposals (RFPs), conceived as short-term research projects, were advertised during March 2005. The application deadline was April 15 and several proposals were received for each of the following RFPs:

RFP1: The Impact of Participating in School Music Programs on Standardized Test Results

Proposals are requested to conduct a short-term quantitative research study of the impact of participating in high or low quality school music programs on standardized test results. Specifically, the proposed study should be designed to investigate the relationship between fourth- and eighth-grade students' end-of-grade test scores and their participation in school music programs recognized as either high or low quality programs. The successful proposal should include a description of: (a) methods by which schools will be differentiated in terms of quality music education programs, (b) process of obtaining end-of-grade test scores as well as other data necessary to produce valid and generalizable results, and (c) methods of data analysis. Additionally, the proposal should include a timeline and a budget, and evidence of prior experiences in executing the procedures to complete the project successfully. The final report is due January 3, 2006.

RFP2: The Importance of Music Education in the Lives of Teenagers

The purpose of this project is to determine the importance of music education in the lives of teenagers based on a content analysis of 1,500 essays. Collected for another project, these essays were written by middle and high school students from all over the United States as they expressed their thoughts and feelings on music education. In particular, we are interested in making connections to the four primary themes of: (a) achievement and success in school, (b) all aspects of a child's growth and development, (c) the uses and functions of music in daily life, and (d) the home, school, and community environments. The proposal should indicate how the researcher intends to conduct the analysis, and should include a timeline and a budget; supporting materials should provide evidence of prior experience using content analysis techniques. The final report is due January 3, 2006.

RFP3: The Impact of a Quality Music Program on K-12 Education

The purpose of this project is to perform short-term qualitative research within a school district recognized for its musical quality. We are interested in obtaining a creative proposal that can identify the primary student achievement and success outcomes caused by music. The study would look at the breadth of possibilities of how music impacts children in elementary and secondary schooling as exemplified in one school district with a quality music program. The study should provide a sorted list of the major outcomes that can be used to focus future research. The supporting qualitative evidence for each outcome's rating must be provided. Summer 2005 is to be used for planning the implementation of the study. The research is to be implemented during Fall 2005. The final report is due January 3, 2006.

Phase I Awards

Christopher M. Johnson, Professor of Music Education and Music Therapy from the University of Kansas, was chosen to conduct RFP1: *The Impact of Participating in School Music Programs on Standardized Test Results*. Patricia S. Campbell, Donald E. Petersen Professor of Music at the University of Washington, was selected to conduct RFP2: *The Importance of Music Education in the Lives of Teenagers*. Final reports on these two projects are due January 3, 2006.

Although several proposals were received for RFP3: The Impact of a Quality Music Program on K-12 Education, ultimately it was decided not to fund this project.

Phase 1: SoL Status Report and Database

The second part of Phase 1 was to prepare a document that would provide the background and context for SoL. This Status Report is accompanied by a Database that will be described subsequently. Following the introductory chapter, the next five chapters (with their authors) are related to the main themes: 2: The Impact of Music Education on Academic Achievement (Hodges & O'Connell), 3: The Impact of Music Education on All Aspects of a Child's Growth and Development (Teachout), 4: The Impact of Music Education on the Child's Self (O'Connell), 5: The Uses and Functions of Music as a Curricular Foundation for Music Education (Haack), and 6: The Impact of Music Education on Home, School, and Community (Asmus). The purpose of these chapters is to review the relevant literature and to discuss implications for learning, for future research, and for policy makers. These review chapters are followed by 7: A Research Agenda to Investigate the Impact of Music Education (Hodges).

A unique feature of the review chapters is that details of relevant research studies are not included in the paper itself, rather they may be found in a Database available at http://www.uncg.edu/mus/soundsoflearning.html or on the IFMR website at www.music- research.org. The advantage of this approach is that the review chapters are focused more on broad conclusions than on supportive detail. This should facilitate understanding for policy makers and others who are interested in the broad conclusions of relevant research. Those who are interested in the specific aspects of particular research studies can find those details in the Database.

The SoL Database is a fully searchable relational database that includes a complete citation for each study (author(s), title, journal, volume, issue, pages), as well as an abstract, and coding with respect to the four major areas of emphasis (e.g., achievement and success in school, etc.). Abstracts have been prepared by chapter authors, their research assistants, or by Dr. O'Connell. Published journal articles and unpublished dissertations are included; data entry is ongoing.

Chapter 7: A Research Agenda to Investigate the Impact of Music Education synthesizes the findings of the previous five chapters. From that synthesis, a research agenda was developed to provide a broad overview of research needed to improve our understanding of the impact of music education. Finally, seven Requests for Proposals were created based on the SoL research agenda. These RFPs are being presented to the music education research community in an effort to recruit experienced researchers to conduct specified studies. Funding from the IMFR, Department of Education, and Grammy Foundation will support these efforts.

PHASE 2

Based on the *SoL Status Report* and Database, and particularly the research agenda, a second round of RFPs was announced on September 1, 2005. Proposals should be submitted by November 1 and research award recipients will be announced December 5, with most final reports due December 1, 2006. A few projects may be given longer timeframes to allow for longitudinal studies or data gathering that may take more time. For complete details, see the concluding section of Chapter 7 or go to http://www.uncg.edu/mus/soundsoflearning.html or http://www.music-research.org.

Concurrent with the recruitment of researchers to conduct studies from Phase 2 RFPs is the dissemination of this document for review and commentary by a panel of selected music educators, including:

> David Circle, President of Music Educators National Conference: The National Association for Music Education; Coordinating Teacher for Blue Valley (KS) School District
>
> Charles A. Elliott, Director of the School of Music, University of Southern Mississippi
>
> Clifford K. Madsen, Robert O. Lawton Distinguished Professor of Music, Coordinator of Music Education/Music Therapy/Contemporary Media, Florida State University

Gary E. McPherson, Zimmerman Professor of Music Education, University of Illinois

Wendy L. Sims, Director of Studies in Music Education, University of Missouri

Peter R. Webster, John W. Beattie Professor of Music Education and Technology, Associate Dean for Academic Affairs and Research, Northwestern University

These experts were asked to provide independent oversight, to identify missing studies in the review chapters, suggest wording changes to more accurately reflect understandings on broad issues, and to nominate items for the research agenda. Suggested RFPs are also welcomed, and these may be added to the third round of RFPs (September, 2006). Their reviews will be included in the second draft of this document.

Following the submission of final reports, all research award recipients from Phases 1 and 2 will meet with the Steering Committee (February 18-19, 2006). This will be a time of information sharing of both completed and in-progress research. Ensuing discussions will focus on integrating this new information into the existing knowledge base as synthesized and analyzed in the SoL Status Report and Database. Also, the group will discuss topics to be included in Phase 3 RFPs.

PHASE 3

Phase 3 RFPs will be announced September 1, 2006. Phase 2 Final Reports are due December 1. Based on these completed studies, a new version of the SoL Status Report and Database will be prepared. This will include a compendium of all the funded research to date that not only provides complete details of the research projects, but also includes a synthesis of this knowledge. Wherever appropriate, broad conclusions will be developed and an updated status report on the impact of music education will be made available. In particular, specific recommendations for policy makers will be emphasized. The compendium will be presented at a Sounds of Learning Summit to be held in Washington, D.C. in February 2007.

CONCLUSION

As stated at the outset, the primary purpose of the SoL project is to determine the impact of music education. Beyond this is the desire to provide policy makers with rigorous, data-based information that will inform decision making. Since the time of Lowell Mason in the early 1800s music educators have been engaged in nearly constant struggle to justify a rightful place for music in the school curriculum. Throughout that time there have been thousands of dedicated music educators who have impacted hundreds of thousands of children in profound and positive ways. Yet, too often music is still marginalized and rarely recognized for the powerful role it should play in a quality education. It would be naïve to assume that the publication of this document will solve all these problems. Nevertheless, there is strong belief that high-quality research, particularly research focused on core issues, will be a significant step forward in placing music in its rightful place in the curriculum.

Appendix W—International Society for Music Education Standing Committee for Advocacy: Mission

This document, shown in Figure W.1, outlines the mission developed by the Advocacy Standing Committee for the International Society for Music Education (and can be found at http://www.isme.org/about-isme/11-advocacy-standing-committee-asc/31-advocacy-standing-committee-asc).

The mission of the Advocacy Standing Committee is to identify and create opportunities to advocate on behalf of music education in international forums through-out the world, emphasizing the importance of including music in the education and life of every young person. To accomplish this mission, the work of the committee should include:

- Planning and offering advocacy sessions at the ISME biennial world Conference;
- Maintaining and updating an advocacy resource page with a variety of materials and relevant links on the ISME website;
- Identifying and publicizing existing advocacy materials in ISME journals and newsletters;
- Serving as a resource for music educators who need assistance in advocating for music education in particular regions and countries;
- Developing closer ties with partner organizations in business, government, and other national associations to coordinate a more international perspective on advocacy; and
- Collecting and sharing successful advocacy efforts from various countries around the world.

Figure W.1 International Society for Music Education Advocacy Standing Committee Mission. Copyright © 2014 ISME All Rights Reserved. Permission to use granted by ISME.

Appendix X—International Society for Music Education Advocacy Blogspot

Log on to this International Society for Music Education web link, given in Figure X.1, to access a variety of documents that support music education advocacy.

(http://official-isme.blogspot.com/search/label/advocacy)

Figure X.1 International Society for Music Education blog posts for advocacy. Copyright © 2014 ISME All Rights Reserved. Permission to use granted by ISME.

Appendix Y—International Society for Music Education Voices of Children

The International Society for Music Education has compiled comments from children all over globe, shown in Figure Y.1 and available from http://www. http://official-isme.blogspot.com/2011/02/advocacy-childrens-voices.html.

- "When I am happy I like to sing those songs that I like."
  Age 8 Hong Kong, China
- "Music makes me aware of who I am. Singing and dancing is a part of my life, so to be able to sing and dance at school makes my life complete."
  Age 17 Namibia
- "Studying music is important because it gives you a good attitude. It gives you a high goal and gives you determination to work hard."
  Age 11 Canada
- "When I hear some lovely music I feel that I can fly."
  Age 6 Hong Kong, China
- "Music has definitely helped me understand myself better."
  Age 15 Australia
- "Me gusta la música porque despierta en mi diferentes sentimientos, y me gusta hacer música con otros chicos porque todos dependemos de todos sea simple o complicada la parte que haya que tocar." [I like music because it arouses in me different feelings. I like playing music with other children because we all depend on each other, no matter how simple or difficult the part we have to play can be.]
  Age 12 Argentina
- "Music is important because it let's kids' brains flow into new experiences and learn in new ways."
  Age 9 United States of America
- "Ich kann ohne Musik nicht leben. Musik bedeutet für mich Spaß und Action. Wenn ich sauer auf meine Eltern oder Schwester bin, dann mach ich mir Musik an und reg mich wieder ab." [I can't live without music. To me music means fun and action. When I am angry with my parents or my sister, music is able to calm me down]
  Age 13 Germany

http://official-isme.blogspot.com/2011/02/advocacy-childrens-voices.html

Figure Y.1 Children's Voices collected by the International Society for Music Education.
Copyright © 2014 ISME All Rights Reserved. Permission to use granted by ISME.

WEBSITES, BOOKS, AND OTHER MEDIA RESOURCES

Appendix Z—Websites for Active Advocacy

Investigate the web links shown in Figure Z.1 for associations actively participating in advocacy for music. Explore the variety of materials and research findings to supplement the ideas and recommendations in this book.

Arts Education Partnership Publications
   http://www.aep-arts.org/resources-2/publications/
ArtsEdge
   http://Artsedge.kennedy-center.org/educators.aspx
ASCAP—The American Society of Composers, Authors and Publishers
   http://www.ascap.com
Champions of Change
   http://Whitehouse.gov/champions/arts-education
Children's Music Workshop
   http://www.childrensmusic-workshopcom/advocacy
Drum Corps International
   http://www.dci.org
GoArts.org
   http://www.goarts.org/

Figure Z.1 Websites for active advocacy.

Grammy in the Schools
    http://www.grammy.org/grammy-foundation/grammy-in-the-schools
Federated State Associations
    http://www.nafme.org/about/federated-state-associations/
Government Agencies and Elected Officials in each state
    http://www.usa.gov/Agencies.shtml#State,_Local,_and_Tribal_Government
International Music Products Association
    http://www.namm.org
Key Federal Education members
    http://www.nafme.org/wp-content/files/2014/06/Key-Federal-Education-Members.pdf
National Assembly of State Arts Agencies
    Nasaa-arts.org/Advocacy/Advocacy-Tools/index.php
Music for All
    http://www.musicforall.org
National Association for Music Education
    http://advocacy.nafme.org/
National School Boards Association
    http://www.nsba.org
Roundtable state of the union response
    http:www.nafme.org/wp-content/files/2014/06/Roundtable-State-of-the-Union-
        Response.pdf
Society for American Music
    http://american-music.org
SupportMusic.com
    http://www.nammfoundation.org/support-music
VH1 Save the Music
    http://www.vh1savethemusic.org/

Figure Z.1 (Continued)

Appendix AA—Websites for National Association for Music Education Federated State Associations

Listed in Figure AA.1 are the web links for the NAfME federated state associations. Use the advocacy materials, blogs, and other resources on these websites to serve as a resource guide to support successful advocacy actions.

The Alabama Music Educators Association
    http://www.alabamamea.org/
The Alaska Music Educators Association
    http://alaskamea.ning.com/
The Arizona Music Educators Association
    http://www.azmea.org/AMEA/
The Arkansas Music Educators Association
    http://www.arkmea.org/
The California Music Educators Association
    http://www.calmusiced.com/
The Colorado Music Educators Association
    http://www.cmeaonline.org/
The Connecticut Music Educators Association
    http://www.cmea.org/

Figure AA.1 Websites for the National Association for Music Education Federated State Associations.

The Delaware Music Educators Association
http://delawaremea.org/
The Washington D C Music Educators Association
https://sites.google.com/site/wdcmeaorg/home
The European Music Educators Association
http://emea.aes.hdso.eportalnow.net/
The Florida Music Educators Association
http://www.flmusiced.org/
The Georgia Music Educators Association
http://www.gmea.org/
The Hawaii Music Educators Association
http://www.hawaiimea.org/
The Idaho Music Education Association
http://www.idahomusiced.org/
The Illinois Music Education Association
http://www.ilmea.org/
The Indiana Music Education Association
http://www.imeamusic.org/
The Iowa Music Educators Association
https://www.iamea.org/
The Kansas Music Educators Association
http://www.ksmea.org/home/index.php
The Kentucky Music Educators Association
http://www.kmea.org/
The Louisiana Music Educators Association
http://www.lmeamusic.org/
The Maine Music Educators Association
http://www.mainemmea.org/
The Maryland Music Educators Association
http://www.mmea-maryland.org/
The Massachusetts Music Educators Association
http://www.massmea.org/
The Michigan Music Education Association
http://www.mmeamichigan.org/
The Minnesota Music Educators Association
http://www.mmea.org/
The Mississippi Music Educators Association
http://www.msmea.org/
The Missouri Music Educators Association
http://www.mmea.net/
The Montana Music Educators Association
http://www.mtmusiced.com/
The Nebraska Music Educators Association
http://nmeanebraska.org/
The Nevada Music Educators Association
http://www.nmeamusic.org/
The New Hampshire Music Educators' Association
http://www.nhmea.org/
The New Jersey Music Educators Association
http://www.njmea.org/
The New Mexico Music Educators Association
http://www.nmmea.com/
The New York State School Music Association
http://www.nyssma.org/
The North Carolina Music Educators Association
http://www.ncmea.net/
The North Dakota Music Educators Association
http://www.ndmea.org/

Figure AA.1 (Continued)

The Ohio Music Education Association
   http://www.omea-ohio.org/
The Oklahoma Music Educators Association
   http://www.okmea.org/
The Pennsylvania Music Educators Association
   http://www.pmea.net/
The Rhode Island Music Education Association
   http://www.rimea.org/
The South Carolina Music Educators Association
   http://scmea.net/
The South Dakota Music Education Association
   http://www.sdmea.net/
The Tennessee Music Education Association
   http://www.tnmea.org/
The Texas Music Educators Association
   http://tmec.org/
The Utah Music Educators Association
   http://umea.us/
The Vermont Music Educators Association
   http://www.vmea.org/
The Virginia Music Educators Association
   http://www.vmea.com/
The Washington Music Educators Association
   http://www.wmea.org/
The West Virginia Music Educators Association
   http://wvmea.tripod.com/
The Wisconsin Music Educators Association
   http://www.wmea.com/
The Wyoming Music Educators Association
   http://www.wyomea.org/

Figure AA.1 (Continued)

Appendix BB—Thoughts on Charter Schools

Past NAfME (formerly the Music Educators National Conference [MENC])
presidents Paul Lehman and Karl Glenn share their perspectives on charter schools and music education classes offered in those schools in Figures
BB.1A and BB.1B.

Appendix CC—Membership of the National Association for Music
Education Music Education Policy Roundtable

Listed in Figure CC.1 are the names of the associations and organizations
that are participating in the Music Education Policy Roundtable.

Paul Lehman's letter, Past MENC President

Lynn:

My understanding of the research is that the alleged advantage of charter schools is by no means as clear-cut as advocates claim. At best the results are mixed—especially when the effects of the many other variables that influence student performance are accounted for. The massive, credible study cited in the attachment below, for example, suggests that most students do worst or no better in charter schools.

If and when some subgroups of kids do better in charter schools, then the logical approach would be to figure out what techniques or conditions cause them to do better and use those techniques or conditions in the public schools—at least for those kids. That makes more sense than building a separate, parallel system that inevitably will serve mostly advantaged students and leave the disadvantaged ones in failed schools. If it's not possible to identify such techniques or conditions, then perhaps the premise that they're better is flawed. In other words, if charter schools turn out to be better, then let's make public schools more like charter schools in their distinguishing respects. But such decisions should be based on evidence rather than emotions. And let's remember that these results will depend entirely on how we define and measure "better." After all, there's more to education that reading and math scores.

In any case, the battle for music education clearly has to be fought all over again in the charter schools. It's tough because their organizational structures are more diffuse and their objectives generally more narrowly focused. Here too it's necessary to assemble coalitions of thoughtful parents, progressive educators, like-minded community leaders, and other allies.

In the final analysis, any kid who doesn't receive a balanced education including music has been cheated regardless of what kind of school he/she went to.

Paul

http://www.npr.org/2013/07/16/201109021/the-charter-school-vs-public-school-debate-continues

Figure BB.1A Letter by past NAfME president Paul Lehman regarding charter schools.

Dear Lynn and All: I recommend two articles, which crystalize and summarize the debate about charters and public schools.

"Charters, Public Schools and a Chasm Between," by Javier C. Hernandez, New York Times, May 11, 2014. This article points out the interactions between charters, private foundation money, and businesses that have exerted great influence on American education.

"Reign of Error," by Diane Ravitch, article by Jonathan Kozol, New York Times, September 26, 2013. As you know, Ravitch was one of the early advocates of the privatization of public education in the 1990's. She has since changed her tune. You be the judge!

I would like to recommend this quote in the New York Times, June 9, 1998 by Sandra Day O'Connor former Supreme Court Justice in her speech at the Games for Change Conference in New York:

"One unintended effect of the 'No Child Left Behind Act,' which is intended to help fund teaching of science and math to young people, is that it has effectively squeezed out civic education because there is no testing for that anymore and no funding for that," she said. "At least half of the states no longer make the teaching of civics and government a requirement for high school graduation. This leaves a huge gap, and we can't forget that the primary purpose of public schools in America has always been to help produce citizens who have knowledge and the skills and values to sustain our republic as a nation, and our democratic form of government."

Accordingly, I always have maintained that the power of nationally uniform curricular standards lies in the testing of them. Nationally uniform testing acts as "product analysis" for measurement and comparison. As the result, states and institutions are under great pressure to improve test schools in line with those subjects to be tested and scored and other knowledge areas and skills diminish automatically in importance.

Figure BB.1B Letter by past NAfME president Karl Glenn regarding charter schools.

The art of music, and the teaching of music, contain much more feeling, imagination, and inspiration than this sort of testing brinkmanship requires. Whether it is public, charter, or religious schools, this presents an opportunity for music education. The public knows this and it values music more on its own terms with wholesome participation according to the level of the student's abilities and talents.

As with the recent NAfME campaign, I believe that music advocacy must emphasize music for its own sake and let the chips fall where they may in this current debate over public vs. charter vs. private schooling. Music is eternal and always has been a necessary part of human nature—it will survive and prosper only if we emphasize this important fact.

Thanks for the opportunity to respond. Karl

Figure BB.1B (Continued)

Current Roundtable Members

Membership in the Roundtable continues to expand. Members are listed below. You can access links to each of their websites by logging on to the NAfME website at the link provided. (http://www.nafme.org/take-action/music-education-policy-roundtable/)

- American Choral Directors Association
- American Orff-Schulwerk Association
- American School Band Directors Association
- American String Teachers Association (Co-founding Member-Group)
- Barbershop Harmony Society
- Chorus America
- College Band Directors National Association
- Drum Corps International
- Education Through Music
- El Sistema USA: A National Alliance of El Sistema Inspired Programs
- Gordon Institute for Music Learning
- Guitar and Accessories Marketing Association
- GRAMMY Foundation
- iSchoolMusic.org
- Jazz at Lincoln Center
- J. W. Pepper & Son (Supporter)
- League of American Orchestras
- Little Kids Rock
- Music for All
- Music Teachers National Association
- Music Publishers Association
- Music Sales Group / MusicFirst (Supporter)
- National Association for Music Education (Co-founding Member-Group)
- National Association of Music Merchants
- National Association of Music Parents
- National Music Council
- Organization of American Kodály Educators
- Percussive Arts Society
- Phi Mu Alpha
- Progressive Music (Supporter)
- Quadrant Arts Education Research
- The Recording Academy
- Strathmore Hall Foundation
- VH1 Save the Music Foundation

Figure CC.1 Members of the Music Education Policy Roundtable.

Appendix DD—United States Military Music Ensembles

Listed in Figure DD.1 are the names of the United States Military Ensembles, accompanied by links to their respective websites.

The President's Own Marine Band. Address:
   http://musiced.about.com/od/musicorganizations/a/usmarineband.htm.
The United States Air Force Band. Address:
   http:///www.usafband.af.mil/education/index.asp.
The United States Army Band. Address:
   http://www.music.army.mil/education/.
The United States Coast Guard Band. Address:
   http://www.uscg.mil/band/Education/SchoolConcerts.asp.
The United States Navy Band. Address:
   http://www.navyband.navy.mil/education.shtml.

Figure DD.1 Websites for the United States Military Ensembles.

NOTES

CHAPTER 1

1. (2014). Advocacy. *New Oxford American dictionary*. http://www.oxforddictionaries. com/us/definition/american_english/advocacy.
2. (2014). Advocacy. *Merriam-Webster's online dictionary*. Website accessed 12/16/ 14. Address: http://www.merriam-webster.com/dictionary/advocacy.
3. Woodside, C. (2014). Telephone interview, C. Woodside, NAfME Assistant Executive Director for Advocacy and Constituency Engagement, The National Association for Music Education, Reston, VA. May 23, 2014.
4. *Teaching Music*. The National Association for Music Education, Reston, VA. Address: http://www.nafme.org/community/societies-and-councils/periodicals/.
5. *Music Educators Journal*. The National Association for Music Education, Reston, VA. Address: http://www.nafme.org/community/societies-and-councils/periodicals/
6. *IWISE: Wisdom on Demand*. Website accessed 12/16/14. Address: http.//www. iwise.com/z9cYd.
7. Birge, E. B. (1966). *History of public school music in the United States*. Music Educators National Conference, Reston, VA, 49.
8. Madsen, C. K. (Ed.). (2000). *Vision 2020: The Housewright symposium on the future of music education*. Music Educators National Conference, Reston, VA, 219–220.
9. Riley, R. W. (1999). *Housewright declaration*. Remarks by U.S. Secretary of Education Richard W. Riley, National Assembly of MENC, Reston, VA. July 13, 1999.
10. (2009). *MENC advocacy activities timeline*. Handout distributed to state and national leadership. Music Educators National Conference, Reston, VA.
11. (2013). Email sent to NAfME members entitled "NAfME spotlight: ArkMEA and NAfME collaborate in successful state-level advocacy effort." National Association for Music Education, Reston, VA. March 16, 2013.
12. Rose, P. (2014). Email update on legislation impacting ArkMEA students and teachers, December 23, 2014.
13. Circle, D. E. (2014). Information submitted by Past NAfME President David Circle in regards to actions by the Kansas Music Educators Association (KMEA). Jean Nye was serving as the KMEA president at that time. February 19, 2014.
14. Luehrsen, M. (2014). Telephone interview, M. Luehrsen, NAMM Foundation Executive Director, International Music Products Association (NAMM). June 11, 2014.
15. (2012). Members of the MENC National Executive Board voted to ratify the Constitution, Bylaws, and Articles of Incorporation on March 5, 2012. The name

of the association was changed from MENC: The National Association for Music Education (abbreviated MENC) to the National Association for Music Education (abbreviated NAfME). Details supplied by Marlynn Likens, Associate Executive Director for NAfME. December 22, 2014.

16. Elementary and Secondary Education Act of 1965, Public Law 107–110, Known as No Child Left Behind (NCLB). Address: http://www2.ed.gov/policy/elsec/leg/esea02/index.html.

17. Yorty Papas, N. P. (2014). Telephone interview, Nicole Yorty Papas, Elementary Music Specialist, Derfelt Elementary School, Clark County School District, Las Vegas, NV. June 24, 2014.

18. Yorty Papas, N. P. (2014). Telephone interview. December 19, 2014.

19. Lautzenheiser, T. (2005). *Music advocacy and student leadership: Key components of every successful music program, a collection of writings.* GIA Publications, Chicago, IL.

20. Benham, J. L. (2011). *Music advocacy: Moving from survival to vision.* Rowman & Littlefield Education, New York, NY.

CHAPTER 2

1. Harvey, P. (1997). Paul Harvey on music education in our public schools. Address: http://itasca.k12.il.us/peacock/encore/travis/musiced.htm.

2. Robinson, K. (2011). *Out of our minds.* Capstone Publishing, Chichester, West Sussex, United Kingdom, 273.

3. Robinson (2011), 249.

4. Robinson (2011), 62.

5. Greene, M. (1995). *Releasing the imagination: Essays on education, the arts, and social change.* Jossey-Bass, San Francisco, CA, 43, 61.

6. Dille, S. (2014). Beyond testing, schools places for growth, learning. *Austin American-Statesman*, A-6. April 29, 2014.

7. Gardner, H. (1990). *Art education and human development.* Getty Publications, Los Angeles, CA, 50.

8. Houston, P. (2007). Keynote speech. 2007 MENC Centennial Celebration and Congress, Coronado Springs Convention Center, Orlando, FL. June 25–26, 2007. MENC: The National Association for Music Education. Paul Houston was serving as the national president for the American Association of School Administrators at the time.

9. Houston (2007).

10. Raessler, K. (2007). Keynote address. *North Carolina Music Educator*, Winter 2007, 11.

11. (2005). Advocacy and the non-educator performer in the music classroom: Position statement. MENC: The National Association for Music Education, Reston, VA. October 2005. Address: http://musiced.nafme.org/about/position-statements/the-non-educator-performer-in-the-music-classroom/.

12. Luehrsen, M. (2014). Telephone interview, M. Luehrsen, NAMM Foundation Executive Director, International Music Products Association (NAMM). June 11, 2014.

13. www.NAfME.org.

14. Woodside, C. (2014). Telephone interview. C. Woodside, NAfME Assistant Executive Director for Advocacy and Constituency Engagement, National Association for Music Education, Reston, VA. May 23, 2014.

15. (2014). Broader Minded Campaign. National Association for Music Education, Reston, VA. Address: http://www.broaderminded.com.

16. Eisner, E. (2002). What the arts teach and how it shows. In *The arts and the creation of mind*. Yale University Press, London, England, 70–92. Available from NAEA Publications. NAEA grants reprint permission for this excerpt from Ten Lessons with proper acknowledgment of its source and NAEA. Address: http://www.arteducators.org/advocacy/10-lessons-the-arts-teach#sthash.3cusW051.dpuf.

17. Hodges, D. (2005). Why study music? *International Journal of Music Education*, 23:2, 111-115. Address: http://ijm.sagepub.com/.

18. Hodges (2005).

19. Shuler, S. C. (2011). Five guiding principles for music education. *Music Educators Journal*, March 2011, 7–9. Address: http.//www.nafme.org/programs/solutions-music-group/meet-the-experts/scott-shuler/.

20. Medina, J. (2008). *Brain rules: 12 principles for surviving and thriving at work, home, and school*. Pear Press, Seattle, WA.

21. Paulnack, K. (2013). First general session keynote address. 2013 Texas Music Educators Association Clinic/Convention, Henry B. Gonzalez Convention Center, San Antonio, TX.

22. Paulnack (2013).

23. Kraus, N. (2014). NAMM Foundation. Address: http://www.nammfoundation.org/educator-resources/biological-benefits-music-education-nina-kraus-phd.

24. Skoe, E., & Kraus, N. (2012). A little goes a long way: How the adult brain is shaped by musical training in childhood. *Journal of Neuroscience*, 32(34), 11507–11510. Address: http://advocacy.nafme.org/all-research/.

25. Jensen, E. (2001). *Arts with the brain in mind*. Association for Supervision and Curriculum Development, Alexandria, VA, 14.

26. Jensen, (2010). How arts and music change the brain. *Kansas Music Review*, Spring 2010, 13–16.

27. Medina (2008).

28. Medina (2008), 69, 49, 71, 95, 121, 169.

29. Elpus, K., & Abril, C. (2011). High school music ensemble students in the United States: A demographic profile. *Journal of Research in Music Education*, vol. 59 no. 2, 128-145, Elpus shared information regarding this study during a telephone interview, December 2, 2014.

30. Elpus (2014).

31. Elpus, L (2011). Music education: Econometric analyses of issues in music education policy. Northwestern University, 2011, 239 pages; 3456550. Address: http://gradworks.umi.com/34/56/3456550.html.

32. Elpus, K. (2014). Telephone interview. December, 2, 2014. Address: http://elpus.net/work.

33. Elpus (2014).

34. Pink, D. A. (2005). *A whole new mind: Moving from the information age to the conceptual age*. Riverhead Books, New York, NY, 1.

35. Pink, D. A. (2009). Legislative update. *Southwestern Musician*, April 2009, 14.

36. Pink, D. A. (2009). Creativity in 21st century workforce preparation, from a whole new mind; special briefing for Texas legislators in the Senate Chamber. January 26, 2009. Address: http://www.tmea.org/assets/pdf/Creativity_in_21st_Century_Workforce_Prep.pdf.

37. Siebert, J. (2014). Music education and 21st century skills. Research Column, Cathy Applefeld Olson. *Teaching Music*, February 2014, 24.

38. Robinson (2011), 2, 273.

39. Luehrsen, M. (2007). Sounds of Learning Conference, Washington, DC, February 22–24, 2007; Education staff briefing at the Senate and House staff hearings, February 22, 2007.
40. McPherson, G. (2007). Speaker at Sounds of Learning Conference, Washington, DC, February 22–24, 2007; Education staff briefing at the Senate and House staff hearings, February 22, 2007.
41. Lehman, P. (2001). Our strategic plans: How are we doing? MENC National Assembly. August 5, 2001. MENC: The National Association for Music Education, Reston, VA, 13.
42. Circle, D. E. (2011). Why music is important to students. *Kansas Music Review*, Spring 2011, 14.

CHAPTER 3

1. Benham (2011).
2. Pink, D. A. (2009). Creativity in 21st century workforce preparation, from a whole new mind; special briefing for Texas legislators in the Senate Chamber. January 26, 2009. Address: http://www.tmea.org/assets/pdf/Creativity_in_21st_Century_Workforce_Prep.pdf.
3. Robinson (2011), 273.
4. Pink (2009).
5. Robinson, K. (2006). Do schools kill creativity? TED Talk. Address: https://www.bing.com/videos/search?q=ken+robinson%2c+ted+talks.
6. Lautzenheiser (2005).
7. U.S. All American Bowl Marching Band. Address: http://www.usarmyallamerican-bowl.com/marching-band-about/.
8. (2005). MENC's the National Anthem Project. Launched with National Association for Music Merchants (NAMM), Jeep and Gibson Foundation. Music Educators National Conference, Reston, VA.
9. (2002). PSA placement and usage report for "Why Music?" radio campaign: Music in Our Schools Month. March 2002. Prepared by JDM & Associates for the National Association for Music Education: MENC. Address: www.nafme.org/?s=psa+announcements.
10. "Why Music?," 2002.
11. National Education Association. Address: http://www.nea.org/.
12. National Association of State Directors of Teacher Education and Certification. Address: http://www.nasdtec.net/?
13. National Association for Music Education State Federated Music Education Association. Address: http://www.nafme.org/about/federated-state-associations/.
14. Texas Music Educators Conference (TMEC). Address: http://www.tmec.org/.
15. Texas Music Educators Association (TMEA). Address: http://www.tmea.org/.
16. Support Music Coalition. NAMM Foundation. Address: https://www.namm-foundation.org/what-we-do/support-music-coalition.
17. International Society for Music Education (ISME). Address: http://www.isme.org/.
18. NAMM Foundation. Address: https://www.nammfoundation.org/.
19. College Band Directors National Association (CBDNA). Address: http://www.cbdna.org/.
20. American Choral Directors Association (ACDA). Address: http://acda.org/.

21. Organization of American Kodály Educators (OAKE). Address: http://www.oake. org/.

22. National Orchestral Association (NOA). Address: http://nationalorchestral.org/.

23. American Orff-Schulwerk Association (AOSA). Address: http://aosa.org/.

24. Music Teachers National Association (MTNA). Address: http://mtna.org/.

25. American Music Therapy Association (AMTA). Address: http://www.musicther-apy.org/.

26. National Association of Schools of Music (NASM). Address: http://nasm.arts-accredit.org/.

27. NAfME Advocacy Groundswell. National Association for Music Education, Reston, VA. Address: http://www.nafme.org/category/advocacy-groundswell-blog/

28. NAMM Foundation, Carlsbad, CA. Address: http://www.nammfoundation.org/.

29. National Endowment for the Arts (NEA). Address: http://arts.gov/.

30. National Art Education Association (NAEA). Address: http://www.arteducators. org/.

31. National Association of Schools of Theatre (NAST). Address: http://nast.arts-accredit.org/.

32. National Association of Schools of Dance Association (NASD). Address: http:// nasd.arts-accredit.org/.

33. Music Education Policy Roundtable. National Association for Music Education. Address: http://www.nafme.org/take-action/music-education-policy-roundtable/.

34. American String Teachers Association (ASTA). Address: http://www.astaweb.com/.

35. Music Education Policy Roundtable. NAfME Address: http://www.nafme.org/ take-action/music-education-policy-roundtable/.

36. Robinson (2011), 76.

37. (2014). Music in Our Schools Month. National Association for Music Education, Reston, VA. Address: http://www.nafme.org/programs/miosm/music-in-our-schools-month-miosm/.

38. MIOSM and advocacy. National Association for Music Education. Address: http:// www.nafme.org/programs/miosm/miosm-and-advocacy/.

39. Bush, B. (2014). Telephone interview, Bruce Bush, Sales and Marketing Manager for Educational Music for Hal Leonard. May 14, 2014.

40. Bush (2014).

41. Music Achievement Council. NAMM Foundation. Address: https://www. nammfoundation.org/educator-resources/music-achievement-council.

42. NAMM Foundation. Address: https://www.nammfoundation.org/.

43. The United States Air Force Band. Address: http:///www.usafband.af.mil/ education/index.asp.

44. The President's Own Marine Band. Address: http://musiced.about.com/od/ musicorganizations/a/usmarineband.htm.

45. The United States Army Band. Address: http://www.music.army.mil/education/.

46. The United States Navy Band. Address: http://www.navyband.navy.mil/education. shtml.

47. The United States Coast Guard Band. Address: http://www.uscg.mil/band/ Education/SchoolConcerts.asp.

48. Achor, S. (2011). *The happiness advantage: The seven principles that fuel success and performance at work.* Virgin Books, United Kingdom, 129–144.

CHAPTER 4

1. (2002). Music education advocacy survey: Quantitative summary. Mailed to membership and data were summarized. MENC: The National Association for Music Education, Reston, VA. January 16, 2002.
2. Einstein quote. Address: http://www.brainyquote.com/quotes/quotes/a/alberteins121993.html.
3. Jensen (2001), 14.
4. Recommendations for content submitted by Oxford reviewer.
5. Neel, M. (2014). Interview, Marcia Neel, Music Education Consultants. June 13, 2014.
6. Benham (2011), 22, 31.
7. Lautzenheiser, T. (2014). Keynote address. Vermont Music Educators 2014 Conference, Killington Grand Resort Hotel, Killington, VA, October 13, 2014.
8. Benham (2011), 22.
9. Woodside (2014).
10. *Grab and go advocacy, school board: Get the message!* National Association for Music Education. Address: http://www.nafme.org/take-action/advocacy-resources/how-to-advocacy-guides/.
11. *Grab and go advocacy, parents: Get the message!* National Association for Music Education. Address: http://www.nafme.org/take-action/advocacy-resources/how-to-advocacy-guides/.
12. *Grab and go advocacy, elementary school principals: Get the message!* National Association for Music Education. Address: http://www.nafme.org/take-action/advocacy-resources/how-to-advocacy-guides/.
13. *Grab and go advocacy, secondary school principals: Get the message!* National Association for Music Education. Address: http://www.nafme.org/take-action/advocacy-resources/how-to-advocacy-guides/.
14. Parsons, B. N. G. (2000). North Carolina coalition for music education. *North Carolina Music Educator*, Spring 2000, 10.
15. National Association for Music Education State Federated Music Education Associations. Address: http://www.nafme.org/about/federated-state-associations/.
16. NAMM Foundation. Address: http://www.nammfoundation.org.
17. World Music Drumming. Address: http://www.worldmusicdrumming.com.
18. Delgado, L. (2006). Advocacy tips, ideas, and strategies. President, MENC Southwestern Division Fall Meeting, Kansas City, MO, 1. July 22–23, 2006.
19. Schmidt, J. E. (2008). An uneasy alliance: Music education and public policy. *VOICE*, January 2008, 15–16. Joan Schmidt was past president for the National School Boards Association at the time.
20. Howell, J. (2002-2003). Advocacy: How do you play the game? President's Column, *Oregon Music Educator*, Winter 2002–2003, 7.
21. Mathews, M. (2014). Lobbyist for Texas Music Educators Association. TMEA Fall College Division Meeting, TMEA Headquarters, Austin, TX. October 10, 2014.
22. Benham, J. L. (2014). Telephone interview, November 12, 2014.
23. Woodside, C. (2014). Meeting, NAfME Executive Director Michael Butera, NAfME Deputy Executive Director and Chief Operating Officer Michael Blakeslee, and NAfME Assistant Director for Advocacy and Public Affairs Chris Woodside. 2014 National Music Education In-Service Conference, Nashville, TN, October 28, 2014.
24. Music Education Policy Roundtable, National Association for Music Education. Address: http://www.nafme.org/take-action/music-education-policy-roundtable/.

25. Music Education Policy Roundtable, National Association for Music Education.
26. Neel, M. (2013). *Making an advocate out of your principal: 10 things you can do Monday!* National Association for Music Education. Address: http://www.nafme.org/wp-content/files/2014/05/How-to-make-an-advocate-out-of-your-principal.pdf.
27. Benham, J. L. (2011). Reporting your progress. *Southwestern Musician*, May 2011, 51.
28. Delgado, L. (2006). Advocacy tips, ideas, and strategies. President, MENC Southwestern Division Fall Meeting, Kansas City, MO, 1. July 22–23, 2006.
29. Benham (2011).
30. Benham (2014).
31. Neel (2014).
32. Benham (2014).
33. Neel (2014).
34. Delgado (2006).
35. *Grab and go advocacy, parents: Get the message!* National Association for Music Education. Address: http://www.nafme.org/take-action/advocacy-resources/how-to-advocacy-guides/.
36. Delgado (2006).
37. TRI-M Music Honor Society, National Association for Music Education. Address: http://www.nafme.org/programs/tri-m-music-honor-society/.
38. Bush (2014).
39. NAMM Foundation. Address: (http://www.nammfoundation.org/why-music-matters/research-briefs-did-you-know).
40. Sletto, J. (2014). Thinking outside the box, *Teaching Music*, January, 2014, 8.
41. Lautzenheiser, T. (1996). Advocacy guidelines, what can educators do., *Teaching Music*, 50–52, October, 1996, 50–52.
42. Benham, (2014). Interview.
43. _____Society for Research in Music Education., National Association for Music Education, Reston, VA. Address: http://www.musiced.nafme.org/srme.
44. What to say. National Association for Music Education. Address: http://www.nafme.org/take-action/what-to-say.
45. NAMM Foundation. Address: http://www.nammfoundation.org.
46. NAMM Foundation.
47. What to do. National Association for Music Education. Address: http://www.nafme.org/take-action/what-to-do.
48. National Association for Music Education State Federated Music Education Associations. Address: http://www.nafme.org/about/federated-state-associations/.
49. (2014). Representative Aycock to receive the TMEA distinguished service award. *Southwestern Musician*, February 2014, 16.
50. (2014). *Southwestern Musician*, 16.
51. Victor, R. (2010). *5 golden rules for music advocacy*. National Association for Music Education. Address: http://www.nafme.org/5-golden-rules-for-music-advocacy/
52. National Association for Music Education. Address: http://www.nafme.org/take-action/music-education-policy-roundtable/.
53. Lautzenheiser, T. (2002). Music advocacy = program success being a music advocate. *EMEA Journal* (European Music Educators Association), Spring 2002, 12–13.
54. https://www.nafme.org/category/advocacy-groundswell-blog/
55. Mathews, M. (2014). Lobbyist for Texas Music Educators Association. TMEA Fall College Division Meeting, TMEA Headquarters, Austin, TX. October 10, 2014.

56. Music in Our Schools Month. National Association for Music Education, Reston, VA. Address: http://www.nafme.org/programs/miosm/music-in-our-schools-month-miosm/

57. National Association for Music Education. Address: http://www.nafme.org/?s=archived+webinars.

58. Advocacy Standing Committee. International Society for Music Education. Address: http://www.isme.org/about-isme/11-advocacy-standing-committee-asc/31-advocacy-standing-committee-asc.

59. Advocacy Articles. International Society for Music Education. Address: http://www.isme.org/advocacy-articles.

60. *Advocacy: Children's voices.* International Society for Music Education. Address: http://official-isme.blogspot.com/2011/02/advocacy-childrens-voices.html.

61. Delgado (2006).

62. Lane, M. (2014). Be proactive, not reactive! North by Northwest column, *Idaho Music Notes*, Winter 2014, 10.

63. Ouren, B. (2007). The MENC position statement on advocacy. *Interval* (Minnesota Music Educators Association), 39–40, 42.

64. Parsons, B. N. G.. (2000). North Carolina coalition for music education. *North Carolina Music Educator*, Spring 2000, 10.

65. Schmidt, J. E. (2008). An uneasy alliance: Music education and public policy. *VOICE*, January 2008, 15–16.

66. Sletto, J. (2014). Thinking outside the box. *Teaching Music*, January 2014, 8.

67. Benham (2011).

68. Zeuch, K. (2013). Student times, extreme choral program makeover, advocacy edition. *Choral Journal*, 53(4), 73–74.

69. Luehrsen (2014).

70. Victor (2010).

CHAPTER 5

1. NAfME was then known as the Music Educators National Conference (MENC).

2. Benham, (2011), 74–75.

3. (2014). MIOSM and advocacy. The National Association for Music Education, Reston, VA. Address: http://www.nafme.org/programs/miosm/miosm-and-advocacy.

4. NAfME was then known as MENC.

5. *Teaching Music*, National Association for Music Education, Reston, VA.

6. *Music Educators Journal*, National Association for Music Education, Reston, VA.

7. Recommendations for content by Oxford reviewer.

8. Hyatt, M. (2007). Keynote address. 2007 MENC Centennial Celebration and Congress, Coronado Springs Convention Center, Orlando, FL. June 25–26, 2007. MENC: The National Association for Music Education.

9. Wis, R. M. (2007). *The conductor as leader: Principles of leadership applied to life on the podium.* GIA Publications, Chicago, IL.

10. Recommendations for content by Oxford reviewer 135.

REFERENCES

ASSOCIATIONS AND ORGANIZATIONS

Achor, S. (2011). *The happiness advantage: The seven principles that fuel success and performance at work*. Virgin Books, United Kingdom, 129–144.

Advocacy articles. International Society for Music Education. Address: www.isme.org/advocacy-articles.

Advocacy: Children's voices. International Society for Music Education. Address: http://official-isme.blogspot.com/2011/02/advocacy-childrens-voices.html.

Advocacy Standing Committee. International Society for Music Education. Address: http://www.isme.org/about-isme/11-advocacy-standing-committee-asc/31-advocacy-standing-committee-asc.

American Choral Directors Association. Address: http://www.acda.org.

American Music Therapy Association. Address: http://www.musictherapy.org/.

American Orff-Schulwerk Association. Address: http://www.aosa.org.

American String Teachers Association. Address: http://www.astaweb.com.

College Band Directors Association. Address: http://www.cbdna.org.

Einstein quote. Address: http://www.brainyquote.com/quotes/quotes/a/alberteins121993.html.

Elementary and Secondary Education Act of 1965, Public Law 107–110, known as No Child Left Behind (NCLB). Address: http://www2.ed.gov/policy/elsec/leg/esea02/index.html.

Grab and go advocacy, elementary school principals: Get the message! National Association for Music Education, Reston, VA. Address: http://advocacy.nafme.org/files/2012/04/get_the_message_elementary_principals.pdf.

Grab and go advocacy, parents: Get the message! National Association for Music Education, Reston, VA. Address:http://www.nafme.org/take-action/advocacy-resources/how-to-advocacy-guides/.

Grab and go advocacy, school board: Get the message! National Association for Music Education, Reston, VA. Address: http://www.nafme.org/take-action/advocacy-resources/how-to-advocacy-guides/.

Grab and go advocacy, secondary school principals: Get the message! National Association for Music Education, Reston, VA. Address: http://www.nafme.org/take-action/advocacy-resources/how-to-advocacy-guides/.

International Society for Music Education. Address: http://www.isme.org.

IWISE: Wisdom on Demand. Website accessed 12/16/14. Address: http.//www.iwise.com/z9cYd.

MIOSM and advocacy. National Association for Music Education, Reston, VA. Address: http://www.Nafme.org/programs/miosm/miosm-and-advocacy/#media.

Music Achievement Council. Address: http://www.namm.org/affliates/music-achievement-council.

Music Education Policy Roundtable. National Association for Music Education. Reston, VA. Address: http://www.nafme.org/take-action/music-education-policy-roundtable/.

Music Educators Journal. The National Association for Music Education, Reston, VA. Address: http://www.nafme.org/community/societies-and-councils/periodicals/.

Music in Our Schools Month. National Association for Music Education, Reston, VA. Address: http://www.nafme.org/programs/miosm/music-in-our-schools-month-miosm/

Music Teachers National Association. Address: http://www.mtna.org.

NAfME Advocacy Groundswell. National Association for Music Education, Reston, VA. Address: http://www.nafme.org/category/advocacy-groundswell-blog/.

NAMM Foundation. Carlsbad, CA. Address: http://www.nammfoundation.org/.

National Art Education Association. Address: http://www.arteducators.org.

National Association for Music Education. Reston, VA. Address: http://www.nafme.org/take-action/what-to-know/all-research/

National Association for Music Education, Reston, VA. Address: http://www.nafme.org/take-action/music-education-policy-roundtable/.

National Association for Music Education, Reston, VA. Address: http://www.nafme.org/take-action/what-to-do.

National Association for Music Education Federated State Associations, Reston, VA. Address: http://www.nafme.org/about/federated-state-associations/.

National Association for Music Education, Reston, VA. Address: http://www.nafme.org/community/elearning/archived-webinars/.

National Association of Schools of Dance Association (NASD). Address: http://nasd.arts-accredit.org/

National Association of Schools of Music (NASM). Address: http://nasm.arts-accredit.org/.

National Association of Schools of Theatre. Address: http://www.nast.arts-accredit.org.

National Association of State Directors of Teacher Education and Certification. Address: http://www.nasdtec.net/.

National Education Association. Address: http://www.nea.org/.

National Endowment for the Arts. Address: http://arts.gov/.

National Orchestral Association. Address: http://www.nationalorchestral.org.

Organization of American Kodaly Educators. Address: http://www.oake.org.

The President's Own Marine Band. Address:http://musiced.about.com/od/music organizations/a/usmarineband.htm.

Society for Research in Music Education, National Association for Music Education, Reston, VA. Address: http://www.musiced.nafme.org/srme.

SupportMusic Coalition, NAMM Foundation, Carlsbad, CA. Address: http://www.nammfoundation.org/what-we-do/support-music-coalition.

Teaching Music. The National Association for Music Education, Reston, VA. Address: http://www.nafme.org/community/societies-and-councils/periodicals/.

Texas Music Educators Association, Austin, TX. Address: http://www.tmea.org.

Texas Music Educators Conference, The Texas state affiliate of NAfME, The National Association for Music Education. Address: http://www.tmec.org/3.html.

TRI-M Music Honor Society. National Association for Music Education, Reston, VA. Address: http://musiced.nafme.org/tri-m-music-honor-society/.

The United States Air Force Band. Address: http:///www.usafband.af.mil/education/index.asp.

The United States Army Band. Address: http://www.music.army.mil/education/.

The United States Coast Guard Band. Address: http://www.uscg.mil/band/Education/SchoolConcerts.asp.

The United States Navy Band. Address: http://www.navyband.navy.mil/education.shtml.

What to say. National Association for Music Education, Reston, VA. Address: http://www.nafme.org/take-action/what-to-say.

World Music Drumming. Address: http://www.worldmusicdrumming.com.

ARTICLES, BOOKS AND WEBSITES

(2002). Music education advocacy survey: Quantitative summary. MENC: The National Association for Music Education, Reston, VA. January 16, 2002.

(2002). PSA placement and usage report for "Why Music?" radio campaign: Music in Our Schools Month. March 2002. Prepared by JDM & Associates for the National Association for Music Education: MENC. Address: http://www.nafme.org/?s=psa+announcements.

(2005). Advocacy and the non-educator performer in the music classroom: Position statement. MENC: The National Association for Music Education, Reston, VA. October 2005. Address: http://musiced.nafme.org/about/position-statements/the-non-educator-performer-in-the-music-classroom/.

(2005). MENC's the National Anthem Project. Launched with the National Association for Music Merchants (NAMM), Jeep and Gibson Foundation. Music Educators National Conference, Reston, VA.

(2009). *MENC advocacy activities timeline*. Handout distributed to state and national leadership. Music Educators National Conference, Reston, VA.

(2012). Members of the MENC National Executive Board voted to ratify the Constitution, Bylaws, and Articles of Incorporation on March 5, 2012. The name of the association was changed from MENC: The National Association for Music Education (abbreviated MENC) to the National Association for Music Education (abbreviated NAfME). Details supplied by Marlynn Likens, Associate Executive Director for NAfME. December 22, 2014.

(2013). Email entitled "NAfME spotlight, ArkMEA and NAfME collaborate in successful state-level advocacy effort." National Association for Music Education, Reston, VA. March 16, 2013.

(2014). Advocacy. *Merriam-Webster*. Website accessed 12/16/14. Address: http://www.merriam-webster.com/dictionary/advocacy.

(2014). Advocacy. *New Oxford American dictionary*. Address: http://www.oxforddictionaries.com/us/definition/american_english/advocacy.

(2014). Broader Minded Campaign. National Association for Music Education, Reston, VA. Address: http://www.broaderminded.com.

(2014). Music in Our Schools Month. The National Association for Music Education. Reston, VA. Address: http://musiced.nafme.org/events/music-in-our-schools-month/.

(2014). Representative Aycock to receive the TMEA distinguished service award. *Southwestern Musician*, February 2014, 51.

Achor, S. (2011). *The happiness advantage: The seven principles that fuel success and performance at work*. Virgin Books, United Kingdom, 129–144.

Benham, J. L. (2011). *Music advocacy: Moving from survival to vision*. Rowman & Littlefield Education, New York, NY.

Benham, J. L. (2011). Reporting your progress. *Southwestern Musician*, May 2011.

Benham, J. L. (2014). Telephone interview, November 12, 2014, 11.

Birge, E. B. (1966). *History of public school music in the United States*. Music Educators National Conference, Reston, VA.

Bush, B. (2014). Telephone interview, Bruce Bush, Sales and Marketing Manager for Educational Music for Hal Leonard. May 14, 2014.

Circle, D. E. (2011). Why music is important to students. *Kansas Music Review*, Spring 2011, 14, 16-17.

Circle, D. E. (2014). Information submitted by Past NAfME President David Circle in regards to actions by the Kansas Music Educators Association (KMEA). Jean Nye was serving as the KMEA president at that time. February 19, 2014.

Delgado, L. (2006). Advocacy tips, ideas, and strategies. President, MENC Southwestern Division Fall Meeting, Kansas City, MO. July 22–23, 2006.

Dille, S. (2014). Beyond testing, schools places for growth, learning. *Austin American-Statesman*, A-6. April 29, 2014.

Eisner, E. (2002). What the arts teach and how it shows. *The arts and the creation of mind*. Yale University Press, London, England, 70–92. Available from NAEA Publications. NAEA grants reprint permission for this excerpt from Ten Lessons with proper acknowledgment of its source and NAEA. Address: http://www.arteducators.org/advocacy/10-lessons-the-arts-teach#sthash.3cusW051.dpuf.

Elpus, L, (2011). Music education: Econometric analyses of issues in music education policy, Northwestern University, 2011, 239 pages; 3456550. Address: http://gradworks.umi.com/34/56/3456550.html.

Elpus, K. (2014). Telephone interview. December, 2, 2014. Address: http://elpus.net/work.

Elpus, K., & Abril, C. (2011). High school music ensemble students in the United States: A demographic profile. *Journal of Research in Music Education*, vol. 59 no. 2, 128-145, Elpus shared information regarding this study during a telephone interview. December 2, 2014.

Gardner, H. (1990). *Art education and human development*. Getty Publications, Los Angeles, CA.

Greene, M. (1995). *Releasing the imagination: Essays on education, the arts, and social change*. Jossey-Bass, San Francisco, CA.

Harvey, P. (1997). Paul Harvey on music education in our public schools. Address: http://itasca.k12.il.us/peacock/encore/travis/musiced.htm.

Hodges, D. (2005). Why study music? National Association for Music Education, Reston, VA. Address: http://advocacy.nafme.org/music-for-musics-sake/.

Houston, P. (2007). Keynote speech. 2007 MENC Centennial Celebration and Congress, Coronado Springs Convention Center, Orlando, FL. June 25–26, 2007. MENC: The National Association for Music Education. Paul Houston was serving as the national president for the American Association of School Administrators at the time.

Howell, J. (2002-2003). Advocacy: How do you play the game? President's Column, *Oregon Music Educator*, Winter 2002–2003, 7, 9.

Hyatt, M. (2007). Keynote address. 2007 MENC Centennial Celebration and Congress, Coronado Springs Convention Center, Orlando, FL. MENC: The National Association for Music Education. June 25–26, 2007.

Jensen, E. (2001). *Arts with the brain in mind*. Association for Supervision and Curriculum Development, Alexandria, VA.

Jensen, E. (2010). How arts and music change the brain. *Kansas Music Review*, Spring 2010, 13–16.

Kraus, N. (2014). NAMM Foundation. Address: http://www.nammfoundation.org/educator-resources/biological-benefits-music-education-nina-kraus-phd.

Lane, M. (2014). Be proactive, not reactive! North by Northwest column, *Idaho Music Notes*, Winter 2014, 10.

Lautzenheiser, T. (1996). Advocacy guidelines, what can educators do. *Teaching Music*, October 1996, 50–52.

Lautzenheiser, T. (2002). Music advocacy = program success being a music advocate. *EMEA Journal* (European Music Educators Association), Spring 2002.

Lautzenheiser, T. (2005). *Music advocacy and student leadership: Key components of every successful music program, a collection of writings*. GIA Publications, Chicago, IL.

Lautzenheiser, T. (2014). Keynote address. Vermont Music Educators 2014 Conference, Killington Grand Resort Hotel, Killington, VA, October 13, 2014.

Lehman, P. (2001). Our strategic plans: How are we doing? MENC National Assembly. August 5, 2001. MENC: The National Association for Music Education, Reston, VA, 13.

Luehrsen, M. (2007). Sounds of Learning Conference, Washington, DC, February 22–24, 2007; Education staff briefing at the Senate and House staff hearings, Russell Building, Rayburn Building, February 22, 2007.

Luehrsen, M. (2007). *Sounds of learning: The impact of music education*. International Foundation for Music Research, Carlsbad, CA. Address: http://performingarts.uncg.edu/mri/research-areas/_files/solproject_final.pdf.

Luehrsen, M. (2014). Telephone interview, M. Luehrsen, Executive Director, International Music Products Association (NAMM). June 11, 2014.

Madsen, C. K. (Ed.). (2000). *Vision 2020: The Housewright symposium on the future of music education*. Music Educators National Conference, Reston, VA, 219–220.

Mathews, M. (2014). Lobbyist for Texas Music Educators Association. TMEA Fall College Division Meeting, TMEA Headquarters, Austin, TX. October 10, 2014.

McPherson, G. (2007). Speaker at Sounds of Learning Conference, Washington, DC, February 22–24, 2007; Education staff briefing at the Senate and House staff hearings, February 22, 2007.

Medina, J. (2008). *Brain rules: 12 principles for surviving and thriving at work, home, and school*. Pear Press, Seattle, WA.

Neel, M. (2013). *Making an advocate out of your principal: 10 things you can do Monday!* National Association for Music Education, Reston, VA. Address: http://www.nafme.org/community/elearning/archived-webinars/advocacy-channel/.

Neel, M. (2014). Interview, Marcia Neel, Music Education Consultants. June 13, 2014.

Parsons, B. N. G. (2000). North Carolina coalition for music education. *North Carolina Music Educator*, Spring 2000, 10.

Ouren, B. (2007). The MENC position statement on advocacy. *Interval* (Minnesota Music Educators Association), 39–40, 42.

Paulnack, K. (2013). First general session keynote address. 2013 Texas Music Educators Association Clinic/Convention, Henry B. Gonzalez Convention Center, San Antonio, TX.

Paulnack, K. (2013). Keynote address for 2013 Texas Music Educators Association for Music Education. *Southwestern Musician*, April 2013, 23–28.

Pink, D. A. (2005). *A whole new mind: Moving from the information age to the conceptual age*. Riverhead Books, New York, NY.

Pink, D. A. (2009). Creativity in 21st century workforce preparation, from a whole new mind; special briefing for Texas legislators in the Senate Chamber. January 26,

2009. Address: http://www.tmea.org/assets/pdf/Creativity_in_21st_Century_Workforce_Prep.pdf.

Pink, D. A. (2009). Legislative update. *Southwestern Musician*, April 2009, 14.

Raessler, K. (2007). Keynote address. *North Carolina Music Educator*, Winter 2007, 11.

Riley, R. W. (1999). *Housewright declaration*. Remarks by U.S. Secretary of Education Richard W. Riley, National Assembly of MENC, Reston, VA. July 13, 1999.

Robinson, K. (2006). Do schools kill creativity? TED Talk. Address: https://www.bing.com/videos/search?q = ken + robinson%2c + ted + talks. March 6, 2014.

Robinson, K. (2011). *Out of our minds*. Capstone Publishing, Chichester, West Sussex, United Kingdom.

Rose, P. (2014). Email update on legislation impacting ArkMEA students and teachers.

Schmidt, J. E. (2008). An uneasy alliance: Music education and public policy. *VOICE*, January 2008, 15–16. Joan Schmidt was past president for the National School Boards Association at the time.

Shuler, S. C. (2011). Five guiding principles for music education. *Music Educators Journal*, March 2011, 7–9. Address: http.//www.nafme.org/programs/solutions-music-group/meet-the-experts/scott-shuler/.

Siebert, J. (2014). Music education and 21st century skills, research column, Cathy Applefeld Olson. *Teaching Music*, February 2014, 24.

Skoe, E., & Kraus, N. (2012). A little goes a long way: How the adult brain is shaped by musical training in childhood. *Journal of Neuroscience*, 32(34), 11507–11510. Address: http://advocacy.nafme.org/all-research/.

Sletto, J. (2014). Thinking outside the box. *Teaching Music*, January 2014, 8.

Victor, R. (2010). 5 golden rules for music advocacy. National Association for Music Education, Reston, VA. Address: http://www.musiced.nafme.org/interest-areas/general-music-education/5-golden-rules-for-music-advocacy.

Wis, R. M. (2007). *The conductor as leader: Principles of leadership applied to life on the podium*. GIA Publications, Chicago, IL.

Woodside, C. (2014). Meeting, NAfME Executive Director Michael Butera, NAfME Deputy Executive Director and Chief Operating Officer Michael Blakeslee, and NAfME Assistant Director for Advocacy and Public Affairs Chris Woodside. 2014 National Music Education In-Service Conference, Nashville, TN, October 28, 2014.

Woodside, C. (2014). Telephone interview, C. Woodside, NAfME Assistant Executive Director for Advocacy and Constituency Engagement, The National Association for Music Education, Reston, VA. May 23, 2014.

Yorty Papas, N. (2014). Telephone interview, Nicole Yorty Papas, Elementary Music Specialist, Derfelt Elementary School, Clark County School District, Las Vegas, NV. June 24, 2014.

Zeuch, K. (2013). Student times, extreme choral program makeover, advocacy edition. *Choral Journal*, 53(4), 73–74.

INDEX

State Board of Education, 19, 21, 30, 39, 50
schools, 1, 2, 16, 19–23, 25–26, 29–31, 33–35, 37–40, 42–45, 47–50, 53–56, 58–66, 68, 70–71, 73, 75–77, 79
  charter schools, 44
  colloquial schools, 44
  elementary schools, 44, 65
  high schools, 29, 33, 44, 65
  home schools, 44
  middle schools, 44, 65
  preschools, 44
  public schools, 17
Senate, 48
  Senators, 3
Shuler, Scott, 26, 28–30
Siebert, Johanna, 35
  Webster Central School Division, New York, 35
Skillpages, 46
Skoe, Erika, 32
Sletto, Johann, 72
social media, 70
Sounds of Learning, 35
South Africa, 28
  shanty-town, 28
  Soweto Kliptown for Youth (SKY), 28
  Soweto Township, 28
superintendents, 40, 44
Supreme Court, 48
Swift, Taylor, 43
symphony orchestra, 40

teachers, teaching, 1–2, 16–17, 19, 22, 24–25, 29–30, 33, 35–36, 39–41, 44–45, 47–51, 53–56, 58–59, 62–63, 68, 70, 75–78
technology, 34

TED Talks, 20, 42
  Sapling Foundation, 20
Testing, 21, 25, 32
  high stakes testing, 1, 21
  pass/fail grading, 24
  Scholastic Assessment Test (SAT), 34
  standardized testing, 21
Texas, 21, 24, 34, 42, 44
  San Antonio, Texas 42
  Texas Music Educators Association (TMEA), 44, 59
  Texas Music Educators Conference (TMEC), 44
Titanic, 31
Toastmasters (*see* community organizations)
Twitter, 46, 66

United States, 5, 44, 49, 51

Vermont Music Educators Association (VMEA), 57
Victor, Richard, 69
Virginia, 46
  Reston, Virginia, 46

Washington, DC, 2–3, 15, 31, 35, 43, 45, 60, 75
Wis, Ramona, 77
Woodside, Chris, 2, 25, 45, 57
World Music Drumming, 58

YouTube, 46

Zeuch, Kyle, 72
Zorro, 51